Northwest Historical Series

I

John Work

The Journal of John Work

A chief-trader of the Hudson's Bay Co. during his expedition from Vancouver to the Flatheads and Blackfeet of the Pacific Northwest

edited, and with account of the Fur Trade in the Northwest, and Life of Work

by

William S. Lewis

and

Paul C. Phillips

Introduction to Second Printing by

Robert Carriker

THE ARTHUR H. CLARK COMPANY

Spokane, Washington

2006

THE ARTHUR H. CLARK COMPANY
P.O. Box 14707
Spokane, WA 99214

ISBN 0-87062-347-8
Library of Congress Control Number 2006923654

Second printing

Contents

Illustrations

Preface

John Work's *Journals* furnish the most extensive records of the fur trade in the Pacific Northwest at the time of its greatest activity. Alexander Ross and Ross Cox described it at the time of its origin but John Work described it when the business had reached maturity.

John Work's *Journals* lack the picturesque settings that characterize the writings of his predecessors, for with him trading and trapping were only serious matters of business. His *Journals*, however, illustrate the geography of the Hudson's Bay Company's activities, and the methods and extent of its trade.

The editors of this *Journal* are indebted for assistance to Mr. T. C. Elliott of Walla Walla, Washington, Mr. John E. Rees of Salmon, Idaho, Miss Jean Bishop of Dillon, Montana, and Miss Hazel Herman of the State University of Montana. The authorship of the notes is indicated by initials.

Introduction to the Second Printing

When the Arthur H. Clark Company published the journal of fur trader John Work in 1923, it was a path-breaking event. Academic publishing, especially in the field of the American West, was not, in the 1920s, the near-exclusive domain of university presses as it is today. The University of Oklahoma Press and the University of Nebraska Press, recognized today as the preeminent publishers of books about the American frontier, did not even begin their work until 1929 and 1941, respectively.[1] Few commercial presses concentrated on western topics, but the Clark Company—then located in Cleveland, Ohio—found that niche in 1902. The idea of placing books into series—that is, organizing titles under a unifying theme, such as western travel or the frontier military—was also a relatively new concept when the Clark company designated John Work's journal of 1831–1832 to be the inaugural volume in their Northwest Historical Series.[2] The book, of which fewer than one thousand copies were printed, for a list price of six dollars, has been available on microfilm since the late 1960s, but this is its first reprinting in book form. It was, and remains, the only publication of John Work's journal for August 18, 1831–July 27, 1832.

[1] The University of Oklahoma Press was only the fourth university press established in the western half of the United States.

[2] A century after its beginning, the Arthur H. Clark Company offered books in twenty-three series, of which the Northwest Historical Series has nineteen volumes. Robert A. Clark and Pat Brunet, *The Arthur H. Clark Company: An Americana Century, 1902–2002* (Spokane: Arthur H. Clark Company, 2003).

By the second decade of the twentieth century only a few fur-trade journals had been edited and published: Alexander Henry, David Thompson, Thomas James, John McLean, Alexander Mackenzie, Ross Cox, and David Douglas. The Arthur H. Clark Company's series Early Western Travels, which began in 1904 under the editorship of Reuben Gold Thwaites, added two more titles, the narratives of Gabriel Franchere and Alexander Ross. But for the most part, there were few published primary documents on the fur trade. Biographies of fur traders were similarly limited in number and centered mostly on William Henry Ashley, Jedediah Smith, or Peter Skene Ogden.[3]

Prior to 1923 none of the fifteen journals written by John Work, arguably the most proficient explorer of the Hudson's Bay Company in the Pacific Northwest, had been widely circulated. Eight segments of Work's journals had been issued between 1909 and 1923, but distribution was limited to subscribers to the *Washington Historical Quarterly* and the *Oregon Historical Quarterly*.[4] Within this limited fraternity of Pacific Northwest historians, Work's journals were appreciated because

[3] Citations for fur-trader journals and narratives are on pages 185–90 of "A Bibliography of the Fur Trade in the Northwest" in *The Journal of John Work*. Many of them have newer editions.

[4] T. C. Elliott, editor, "Journal of John Work, April 30th to May 31st, 1830," *Oregon Historical Quarterly* 10 (1909): 296–313; "Journal of John Work, November and December, 1824," *Washington Historical Quarterly* 3 (1912): 200; "Journal of John Work, Covering Snake Country Expedition of 1830–31," *Oregon Historical Quarterly* 12 (1912): 363–71 and 14 (1913): 280–314; "Journal of John Work, June–October 1825," *Washington Historical Quarterly* 5 (1914): 83–115; "Journal of John Work, September 7–December 14, 1825," *Washington Historical Quarterly* 5 (1914): 163–91; "Journal of John Work, December 15, 1825, to June 12, 1826," *Washington Historical Quarterly* 5 (1914): 258–87; "Journal of John Work, July 5–September 15, 1826," *Washington Historical Quarterly* 6 (1915): 26–49; William S. Lewis and Jacob A. Meyers, editors, "Journal of a Trip from Fort Colville to Fort Vancouver and Return in 1828," *Washington Historical Quarterly* 11 (1920): 104–14; Leslie M. Scott, editor, "John Work's Journey from Fort Vancouver to Umpqua River, and Return, in 1834," *Oregon Historical Quarterly* 24 (1923): 238–68.

they added a new voice to those of Gabriel Franchere, Alexander Ross, and Ross Cox—the men Elliott Coues once dubbed the "three synoptic writers of Astoria," a clever reference to Gospel writers Matthew, Mark, and Luke—each of whom told similar stories about the idiosyncrasies of Columbia River travel and near-constant encounters with Indians. Other journal segments presented by the state historical society quarterlies covered Work's travels from the mouth of the Columbia River to Canada's lower Fraser River and his meanderings between Fort Vancouver and the Umpqua River in Oregon.

Work's journal from August 18, 1831, to July 27, 1832, however, had never been published. It comprised not only Work's most extensive writing it also offered continuous insights into both the work routines of the traders and the policies of the Hudson Bay Company. By this time in his career, Irish-born John Work bore the responsibilities of being a chief trader and, just as important, he was the successor to Peter Skene Ogden as leader of the renowned Snake River Brigade. Work's description of streams and landmarks encouraged scholars to locate and study early maps of the Oregon Country. Where exactly could be found on the map rivers named Walla Walla, Clearwater, Clark's Fork, Blackfoot, John Day, and Salmon? Where did the Blackfeet and the Nez Perce reside? What was the geographic relationship among forts Vancouver, Colville, and Nez Perce?

To bring this important journal publication to fruition, Arthur H. Clark contracted with Paul Chrisler Phillips, a professor at the State University of Montana at Missoula.[5] The original Work journal for this edition resided in the British

[5] Phillips announced on April 3, 1922, when he submitted the preliminary manuscript, that "The President of the University of Montana told me that he would be willing to O.K. an order for two hundred dollars [*sic*] worth of the books when they are published." Paul C. Phillips to Arthur H. Clark Co., April 3, June 16, July 19, and August 15, 1922, in Arthur H. Clark Company archives.

Columbia Archives at Victoria on Vancouver Island. There were also at least four handwritten copies available. In 1878 some 240 pages of John Work's journals, then still in the possession of the Work family, were transcribed for Hubert Howe Bancroft.[6] Thirty years later, after the journals had been donated to the British Columbia Provincial Archives, the archivist, R. E. Gosnell, prepared an abstract for the Canadian National Archives and the Hudson's Bay Company Archives.[7] He also sent a copy to the premier historian of the Pacific Northwest, Professor Edmond S. Meany of the University of Washington.[8] Phillips decided to rely on Meany's 1908 abstract, double-checking it against the Bancroft manuscript.

A professor at the State University of Montana since 1911, Phillips had a single book to his credit, his revised doctoral dissertation at the University of Illinois, *The West in the Diplomacy of the American Revolution*.[9] He was no stranger to the library, however, and he knew well the historical literature of Montana, Idaho, Washington and Oregon, especially the diverse

---

[6] Hubert Howe Bancroft (1832–1918) came to San Francisco, California, in 1852 to establish a bookselling and publishing firm. The History Company, as it was called, also gathered an estimated sixty thousand manuscripts, personal narratives, and biographies and became the foundation for Bancroft's thirty-nine volume *History of the Pacific States of North America* (1885–1890). Since 1905 the collection has been housed at the University of California at Berkeley.

[7] R. Edward Gosnell (1860–1931) came to British Columbia from Quebec in 1888 to be a newspaperman. He became the first provincial librarian of British Columbia in 1893 and, later, he served as the first provincial archivist. Gosnell annually prepared the *Year Book of British Columbia and Manual of Provincial Information* (Victoria, B.C.: Authority Legislative Assembly, 1897–1914) and he gained recognition for his *History of British Columbia* (Chicago: Hill Binding Co., 1906; reprinted, Vancouver and Victoria: British Columbia Historical Association, 1913). He was co-author, with Robert H. Coats, of *James Douglas* (Toronto: Morang & Co., 1908; reprinted, Toronto: Oxford University Press, 1926). See Terry Eastwood, "R. E. Gosnell . . . and the Founding of the Provincial Archives of British Columbia, 1894–1919," *BC Studies* no. 54 (1982): 38–62.

[8] See Kent D. Richards, "Edmond S. Meany: 1862–1935," *Arizona and the West* 17 (1975): 201–4.

[9] Paul C. Phillips, *The West in the Diplomacy of the American Revolution* (New York: Russell & Russell, 1913).

aspects of the fur trade.[10] For this project Phillips also needed to "know the territory." It was imperative that Work's references to his companions, the landmarks he encountered, and the Inland Northwest watercourses he traveled be identified with accuracy. Under the circumstances, Phillips sought the advice of several persons who possessed supporting information.

As early as 1921 William Stanley Lewis, a Spokane attorney who had represented the Colville and Okanogan tribes in court and before the United States House of Representatives Indian Affairs Committee, joined Phillips as the co-editor for the project. Lewis, who had two books to his credit, benefited from his association with the Spokane Public Museum, the Spokane Pioneer Society, and the Eastern Washington Historical Society, of which he was a founding secretary. Three years earlier he had co-edited Work's 1828 journal of a trip from Fort Colville to Fort Vancouver for the *Washington Historical Quarterly*.[11]

Phillips recruited several others to assist him in writing footnotes to the journal entries. He assigned to each footnote the initials of the author. T. C. Elliott, of Walla Walla, Washington, served as Phillips's chief informant. Among Elliott's credits was a book on explorer David Thompson. Between 1909 and 1913, Elliott edited several portions of Work's jour-

[10] Paul Chrisler Phillips (1883–1956) came to the State University of Montana at Missoula in 1911 as chair of the history department—and its only member! He remained department chair until 1937 when he became vice president of the university. By all accounts he was the university's most distinguished historian during the first half of the twentieth century. See Merrill G. Burlingame, "Paul Chrisler Philips: 1883–1956," *Arizona and the West* 24 (1982): 201–4.

[11] William S. Lewis, *The Case of Spokane Garry* (Spokane: Bulletin of the Spokane Historical Society, 1907, and reprint, Fairfield, Wash.: Ye Galleon Press, 1987); editor, with Naoijro Murakami, *Ranald MacDonald: The Narrative of His Early Life on the Columbia Under the Hudson's Bay Company* (Spokane: Inland-American Printing, 1923; reprinted, Portland: Oregon Historical Society Press, 1990); editor, with Jacob A. Meyers, "Journal of a Trip from Fort Colville to Fort Vancouver and Return in 1828," *Washington Historical Quarterly* 11 (1920): 104–14.

nals for both the *Oregon Historical Quarterly* and the *Washington Historical Quarterly*.[12] Another aide, John E. Rees of Salmon, Idaho, had equally worthy credentials. For seventeen years Rees lived among the Shoshone Indians as post trader for the Lemhi Indian Agency. Subsequent to that he taught high school in Salmon, Idaho, and published *Idaho: Chronology, Nomenclature, Bibliography*.[13]

Jacob A. Meyers may not have been well known in the small circle of fur-trade historians, but he certainly knew from personal experience the territory of northeastern Washington traversed by Work. He also owned a collection of pioneer photographs dating from 1885. His writings included several articles in the *Washington Historical Quarterly*, including a journal by John Work that he co-edited with William S. Lewis.[14] Two women identified Montana place-names for Phillips: Miss Hazel F. Herman of Missoula, Montana, and Miss Jean Bishop of Dillon, Montana. Their qualifications have been obscured by the passage of time. Evidence seems to suggest that Miss Herman was a teacher, though not at

[12] Thompson Coit Elliott (1862–1943) was an investment banker. T. C. Elliott, *David Thompson, Pathfinder, and the Columbia River* (Kettle Falls, Wash.: Scimitar Press, 1911). See note 4 for Elliott's publications on John Work.

[13] John E. Rees (1868–1928), *Idaho: Chronology, Nomenclature, Bibliography* (Chicago: W. B. Conkey Co., 1918; reprinted, Seattle: Shorey Book Store, 1965 and 1970). Unpublished manuscripts and letters by Rees are at Idaho State University.

[14] Jacob Allen Meyers (1855–1925) was born at his family's home at Meyers Falls, located three miles east of Kettle Falls on the Columbia River. Workers from the Hudson's Bay Company post at Fort Colville established a gristmill at Meyers Falls in 1826. William S. Lewis and Jacob A. Meyers, editors, "Journal of a Trip from Fort Colville to Fort Vancouver and Return in 1828," *Washington Historical Quarterly* 11 (1920): 104–14; Jacob Allen Meyers, "Jacques Raphael Finlay," *Washington Historical Quarterly* 10 (1919): 163–67; "Finan McDonald: Explorer, Fur Trader and Legislator," *Washington Historical Quarterly* 13 (1922): 196–208; F. W. Howay, William S. Lewis and Jacob A. Meyers, editors, "Angus McDonald: A Few Items of the West," *Washington Historical Quarterly* 8 (1917): 188–229. The photographs taken by Jacob Meyers are in the Lee Cagle Photograph Collection (L87–149) of the Northwest Museum of Arts and Culture in Spokane, Wash.

the university. It is possible that Miss Bishop was a reference librarian, perhaps with the State Normal College at Dillon (University of Montana, Western). Each of the analysts contributed local expertise or perspective; sometimes their views challenged ideas held by Phillips.[15]

Editing and publishing the journal of John Work as a cooperative effort seemed sensible because in the 1920s the field of fur trade history attracted few professional historians.[16] The most comprehensive treatment of the fur trade was Hiram Martin Chittenden's *The American Fur Trade of the Far West* (1902). To achieve his result, Chittenden scrounged through "a half-carload" of fur-company records that were covered, he complained, "with at least three-fourths of the coal iron dust of St. Louis." Since he had neither an index to guide him nor an archivist to assist him, he termed the effort an "appalling task."[17] But the result was a triumph in three volumes, notwithstanding certain limits. The book tended to emphasize fur trade companies, for example, especially those headquartered in St. Louis. The personal stories of the men of the fur trade were relegated to a separate section. John Work was nowhere acknowledged. Chittenden used newspaper records extensively, but he was unaware of many original sources, especially journals written by participants. Interestingly, it took nearly six decades for another historian

[15] For examples, see footnotes 173, 175, 176, and 179.

[16] Dale L. Morgan, "The Fur Trade and Its Historians," *American West* 3 (1966): 28–35, 92–93.

[17] Hiram M. Chittenden, *The American Fur Trade of the Far West: A History of the Pioneering Trading Posts and Early Fur Companies of the Missouri Valley and the Rocky Mountains and of the Overland Commerce with Santa Fe*, 3 vols. (New York: F. P. Harper, 1902). New York City lawyer Stallo Vinton added authoritative footnotes to a new edition in 1935, which has been reissued, usually in two volumes, in 1954, 1976, and 1986. Chittenden's comments are from *H. M. Chittenden: A Western Epic* (Tacoma, Wash.: State Historical Society, 1961): 81–83.

to generate a multi-volume history of the fur trade, and that person was none other than Paul Chrisler Phillips whose *The Fur Trade* (1961) is considered a major contribution to the field.[18] Thus, the publication of *The Journal of John Work* in 1923 had an important impact on fur-trade historiography. Henceforth, fur trade historians would actively seek out the journals of fur traders and put a human face on a gritty business. In addition, Paul Phillips began his inquiry into a subject that would result in the second-most-referenced title in that field.[19]

The *Mississippi Valley Historical Review*, the most important quarterly in the field of American history at the time, called the Work journal "highly interesting" and "a distinct contribution to the history of the fur trade and to the history of the northwest in general." The two introductory chapters written by Phillips received special praise, elevating the book to the status of a "real addition to the literature of the subject." The introduction received special praise, which is not surprising since it contained over one hundred footnote references. The *Catholic Historical Review* also admired the introduction, thinking it probably "the best short account available."[20] Phillips' mini-biography of John Work essentially introduced

[18] Paul Chrisler Phillips, *The Fur Trade*, 2 vols. (Norman: University of Oklahoma Press, 1961). Phillips wife, Alice, and J. W. Smurr, a former student and colleague, completed work on the book after Phillips's death in 1956.

[19] Phillips devoted himself to learning more about the fur trade after he edited John Work's journal, and by the end of 1931 he believed he was close to a finished manuscript. However, in the mid-1930s the Hudson's Bay Company released previously unobtainable records and Phillips found, to his regret, that the grand story he was writing would need a revision. He died in 1956 without finishing the project. Paul C. Phillips to Arthur H. Clark Co., December 3, 1931, Arthur H. Clark Company archives.

Paul C. Phillips wrote one book and edited or co-edited five books during his academic career at the State University of Montana, 1911–1937 and 1946–1954. Among the graduate students he mentored were United States senator Mike Mansfield and Montana Historical Society director and University of Montana history professor K. Ross Toole. Two additional books by Phillips were published posthumously.

[20] *Mississippi Valley Historical Review* 10 (1924): 468–69; *Catholic Historical Review* 3 (1924): 621.

the Hudson's Bay Company operative to the scholarly community of fur-trade historians. It would be twenty years more before a biography of Work would appear, and even then the author, recognizing its shortcomings, characterized his own work as only "somewhat detailed."[21]

The remainder of Work's journals were published after 1923, sometimes verbatim, but mostly as either a summary or an extract. The Columbia River journals of John Work for 1823–1824 were published in 1929.[22] Work's 1825 travel journals from Fort George to Fort Vancouver appeared in 1944.[23] The journals recounting his experiences with the California Brigade in 1832 and 1833 were published between 1944 and 1945, as were Work's journals about his journey up the Northwest Coast in 1835.[24] Finally, in 1971 a second journal of John Work's affiliation with the Snake River Brigade was edited and published.[25] Together with the journals published prior to 1923, already noted, and this publication, the journals of John Work are completely published.

Robert Carriker
Gonzaga University
February 2006

[21] Henry Drummond Dee, "An Irishman in the Fur Trade: The Life and Journals of John Work," *British Columbia Historical Quarterly* 7 (1943): 229–70.

[22] Walter N. Sage, editor, "John Work's First Journal, 1823–1824," *California Historical Association Report* (1929): 21–29; Walter N. Sage and T. C. Elliott, editors, "Governor George Simpson at Astoria in 1824," *Oregon Historical Quarterly* 30 (1929): 106–10.

[23] Nellie B. Pipes, editor, "The Journal of John Work, March 21–May 14, 1825," *Oregon Historical Quarterly* 45 (1944): 138–46.

[24] Alice Bay Maloney, editor, *Fur Brigade to the Bonaventura: John Work's California Expedition, 1832–1833, for the Hudson's Bay Company* (San Francisco: California Historical Society, 1945); Henry Drummond Dee, editor, *The Journal of John Work, January to October 1935* (Victoria: C. F. Banfield, 1945).

[25] Francis D. Haines Jr., editor, *The Snake Country Expedition of 1830–1831: John Work's Field Journal* (Norman: University of Oklahoma Press, 1971).

The Journal of John Work

The Fur Trade in the Northwest

The American fur trade began with the first explorations of the North Atlantic coast.[1] This beginning was at a time when Europe was seeking new materials for shoes, hats, and clothing. An abundance of deer promised leather with which to make comfortable shoes to take the place of the heavy wooden ones or to supply those who were barefoot. The beaver and muskrat colonies were able to furnish vast numbers of pelts with which to provide all classes with serviceable and handsome hats. Other fur bearing animals gave their skins to add to the comfort and beauty of the European's dress.

During the seventeenth and eighteenth centuries French and British traders pushed the fur trade back from the Atlantic coast into the basin of the St. Lawrence and the Great Lakes, along the shores of Hudson's Bay, and even to the country bordering on the Ohio and Mississippi Rivers.[2] On the Pacific coast

---

[1] "There are in these partes most delicate and rare furres. . ." *Reports of Ye Contrie Sr. Humphrey Gilbert goes to discou* in Colonial Office Records vol. i, No. 2. Copy in Canadian Archives. *A Discourse of the necessitie . . . of planting English colonies upon the North partes of America* gives an account of martens, beavers, foxes, blacke and white. *Hakluyt Collections*, 89. Thomas Heriot, a follower of Raleigh's reported in 1586: "Furres all along the sea coast there are great store of otters which will yield good profit." *Ibid.*, viii, 348.

[2] For accounts of the French and British fur trade in the seventeenth and eighteenth centuries see Biggar (H. P.) *Early Trading Companies of New France*, University of Toronto *Studies in History*, 1901, and Willson (Beckles) *The Great Company*, Toronto, 1899.

too, Bering, a Dane in the service of the Russian czars, about the middle of the eighteenth century, gave a great impetus to the trade in sea otters. His successors catered to the vanity of Chinese mandarins with immense profit to themselves. So eager were traders to secure these valuable and beautiful furs that the sea otter long ago became practically extinct.[3]

In spite of the vast trade in furs the Columbia River basin and the valley of the upper Missouri remained untouched and almost unknown to white traders and trappers until after the opening of the nineteenth century. The streams of these mountainous regions abounded in beaver.[4] The pelts were not so large and heavy as those east of the mountains but they were dark in color and rich in texture.[5] Hardly less numerous were the otters whose heavy, dark-brown furs were prized by Russians and Chinese next to those of the sea otter. Bears, wolves, lynx, fishers, muskrats, and foxes, mostly of the red and cross varieties also furnished pelts to make up the trapper's toll.

Along the eastern slope of the Rockies began the great buffalo range of the Northwest.[6] Countless thousands of these animals furnished the Sioux, the

[3] For Bering see Golder (F. A.) *Russian Expansion on the Pacific*, 1641-1850, Cleveland, 1914.

[4] Peter Skene Ogden who was trapping and trading in the Snake River country in 1825-1826 reported the discovery of "a country richer in beaver than any they have ever seen." This country was seventeen days travel from Fort Vancouver on the Columbia. Chief factor McLoughlin to Governor Simpson of the Hudson's Bay Company, Fort Vancouver, August 18, 1826. McLeod (J.) *Journals*, in Canadian Archives, 69.

[5] In 1826 McLoughlin wrote that the beaver from Snake River country the past year were "as good as those east of the mountains." *Ibid.* In 1830 he wrote that "Columbia beaver sells higher per skin than any in America." Fort Vancouver, February 1, 1830, in McLeod *Journals*, 124.

[6] Trexler (H. A.) *Buffalo Range of the Northwest*, in *Mississippi Valley*

Blackfeet, the Crows, and even the tribes west of the continental divide with food, clothing, and shelter. Buffalo meat saved many a white trapper from starvation, and buffalo robes became the currency by which the Indian of the plain paid for the white man's weapons, trinkets, and liquors.

This rich fur country remained undeveloped because abundant supplies could be obtained in more accessible regions. Routes of exploration and of trade crossed the continent either to the south or to the north.[7] The Columbia River was unknown until near the close of the eighteenth century, and even after its discovery it was long believed that the falls and rapids made it a difficult route to the interior. The coast ranges also appeared to offer an almost inpenetrable barrier to any trail leading eastward.

From the east the French were slow to go far west of the Mississippi and the Great Lakes. They early discovered the lower Missouri and some of them thought that it made a road almost to the Pacific.[8] The fur trader believed, however, that its upper course traversed only barren plains inhabited by savage and poverty-stricken Indians whose only food and shelter came from the immense herds of buffalo. Since there was as yet no market for buffalo robes he left these Indians alone. From the western shores of Lake Superior French explorers and traders followed the water routes towards the Northwest through the Lake of the Woods

Historical Review, vii, No. 4, 348-362, gives an account of the size of the buffalo herds and of their importance.

[7] The Spaniards had long before the nineteenth century established regular communication between the Gulf of Mexico and California. Alexander Mackenzie crossed the continent to the north in 1793.

[8] Thwaites (R. G.) *Rocky Mountain Exploration*, New York, 1904, 26.

to Lake Winnipeg, and ultimately to the Rocky Mountains. A rich trade in furs diverted them from the treeless plains to the southwest through which flowed the upper Missouri.

Indian stories of a river that emptied itself into a great salt lake where dwelt white men with beards reached the ears of these French traders. One of them, Pierre Gaultier, Sieur de Varannes de la Verendrye by name, was greatly interested, and he questioned the Indians sharply for all their information.[9] He thought first that the best road to the Pacific lay to the north and west but in 1738 decided to try the route to the southwest. He had obtained no assistance from the French government beyond a grant of the monopoly of the fur trade and depended upon partners and creditors for equipment.[10] Accompanied by two sons, Francois and Louis Joseph, with a party of about fifty Indians and Frenchmen, he made a journey to the Mandans on the Missouri. From there he could not go on and, after hearing other stories of the lake with bitter water, he returned to Fort de la Reine, a short distance west of the present city of Winnipeg.[11]

In 1742 Verendrye sent his two sons on a new attempt to find the western sea. After dreary wanderings across the Dakota plains they saw the mountains on January 1, 1743. Perhaps their eyes gazed upon the Black Hills of South Dakota but more likely they had gone up the little Missouri, across southeastern Montana and were within range of the Bighorn Mountains.[12] Here

---

[9] *Ibid.* DeLand. *The Verendrye Explorations and Discoveries*, in *South Dakota Historical Collections*, Pierre, South Dakota, 1914, vii.

[10] *Ibid.*, 140.

[11] *Ibid.*, 286.

[12] The old belief that the Verendryes saw the Rocky Mountains near the

the threat of Indian war and perhaps discouraging reports of what lay beyond induced the party to return.

The Verendryes planned to renew their explorations in the far west, hoping to open trade with the Indians, and to establish a line of posts that would ultimately lead to the "Sea of the West." The elder Verendrye was granted a monopoly of the far western trade and this aroused the jealousy of rival traders. His creditors harassed him and so many difficulties did he encounter that he could not return to the west before death overtook him in 1749. Soon after this his sons were deprived of his grants and an officer of the royal army was commissioned to find the western sea. The French and Indian War stopped all expeditions of discovery and in 1763 New France passed into British hands, and Louisiana came under the control of Spain.

After the overthrow of French power in America British traders sought for themselves a monopoly of the fur trade. They had already powerfully entrenched themselves in the fur country. In 1670 the Hudson's Bay Company had obtained a charter granting it a monopoly of the fur trade in the basin of Hudson's Bay called Rupert's Land.[13] This charter provided for the continuance of exploration in America but the company was content with the profits arising from trade along the shores of its empire and for a century made little effort to extend its dominion.[14] French traders con-

present Helena, Montana (*Contributions to the Historical Society of Montana*, Helena, Montana, 1902, i, 278) is discredited. The discovery of the Verendrye plate near Pierre, South Dakota, proves that the party did not come so far north as Helena. The most detailed account of the Verendrye expeditions is in the *South Dakota Historical Collections*, vii.

[13] Copy of this charter is in Willson (Beckles) *The Great Company*, Appendix.

[14] "Canadian adventures have annually increased in the upland country,

trolled the trade to the south and west, but there was enough left to yield the company large profits.

At the close of the French and Indian Wars, English and Scotch traders flocked to Montreal and began to struggle for a control of the Great Lakes trade. Alexander Henry, a bold and resourceful adventurer was one of the first to penetrate the region west of Lake Superior.[15] He was closely followed by the erratic and hot tempered Peter Pond[16] and by the shrewd brothers, Thomas and Joseph Frobisher.[17] With the end of the old French system of monopolies French traders also began to strike for a share of this lucrative trade and a bitter rivalry began. Traders furnished great quantities of rum to the Indians whose activities as hunters were thereby reduced. Prices of furs went up to unheard of heights, violence in the fur land was common, and many merchants were ruined.[18]

In 1779 an agreement was formed by a number of merchants at Montreal to pool the traffic but this agreement lasted only two years. In 1783 or 1784 a number of Montreal merchants entered into an agreement for

much to their own emolument, and the great loss of the Company: who it may be said, are sleeping at the edge of the sea, without spirit and without vigour or inclination to assert that right. . . It is true, they have at this time a few establishments in the interior country: but these are carried on in such a languid manner, that their exertions have hitherto proved inadequate to the purpose of supplanting their opponents." Umfreville (Edward) *Present State of Hudson's Bay*, London, 1790, 71. "The Hudson's Bay Company for many years did not go beyond the shores of Hudson's Bay; but the natives came down from all parts." Dodds (James) *Hudson's Bay Company, its Position and Prospects*, London, 1866, 14.

15 Henry (Alexander) *Travels and Adventures in Canada and the Indian Territories 1760-1776*, New York, 1809, 253.

16 *Ibid.*, 252. Pamphlet on *Origin and Progress of Northwest Company*, London, 1811, describes Pond.

17 Henry, *opus citra*, 253.

18 Davidson (G. C.) *The Northwest Company*, Berkeley, 1918, 9.

five years under the name of the Northwest Company. All the traders were not at first included and competition continued until 1787 by which time all the important merchants of Montreal were brought into the partnership.[19]

The formation of the Northwest Company forced the Hudson's Bay Company to expand westward or lose the trade with the western Indians which had grown up after the expulsion of the French. Both began to push their explorations and to establish posts farther and farther westward. Towards the end of the eighteenth century each had traders on the upper Missouri.[20] In 1804 the Northwest Company made a resolute attempt to get control of this trade. It sent out an expedition under the command of Francois Antoine Larocque to win over the Sioux and Crow Indians. Larocque's party spent the winter in the Mandan villages near which Lewis and Clark also had their camp. There he obtained few furs and in 1805 went past the Mandans over to the Powder River, thence to the Littlehorn, the Bighorn, and finally to the Yellowstone, striking it near Pryor's Fork. Larocque purchased more than a hundred beaver skins and offered induce-

[19] *Ibid.*, 10-11. Roderick McKenzie, *Sketch of History of the Northwest Company*, Masson Collection v. "Peter Pond who was not satisfied with the share allotted him . . . accordingly he and another gentleman Mr. Peter Pangman, who had a right to be a partner but for whom no provision had been made, came to Canada with a determination to return to the country if they could find any persons to join. . . Mr. Pangman prevailed on Mr. Gregory and Mr. McLeod to join." Pond soon deserted to the Northwest Company. See also Davidson, *opus citra*, 47.

[20] McKenzie (Charles) *Journal of Second Expedition to the Mississouri*, [sic] 1805, Masson Collection, writes: "In the course of our first trip to the Mississouri having seen several Rocky Mountain Indians we made inquiries of the state of the country regarding trade and learned that beaver were as numerous in their rivers as buffaloes were in the plains. Planned

ments to the Crows to begin hunting for his company.[21] The United States government, however, refused to allow this trade to continue within its borders[22] and the Northwest Company then continued its western expansion along a more northern route.

The work of carrying the British fur trade to the Pacific was entrusted to a group of able men, the most notable of whom were David Thompson, Alexander Henry Jr., and Daniel W. Harmon.[23] Thompson was not really a fur trader. He was a scientist and explorer. His peculiar genius was not appreciated by the Hudson's Bay Company and he left its employ in 1797 to enter the service of the Northwest Company. He was entrusted with the task of marking the line of the forty-ninth parallel to the Rocky Mountains and of reporting on the resources of the country to the north of this line and also of the region beyond the mountains. It appears that possibly as early as 1801 the Northwest Company had planned to extend its trade beyond the Rockies to the Pacific.[24]

It was not until 1807 however, that Thompson actually crossed the Rockies and reached the headwaters of the Columbia. The next spring he traded along the Kootenai River in what is now northwestern Montana.[25]

---

to start trade. Mr. Larocque was appointed to carry out this plan. Fall 1805 reports H. B. C. traders in Missouri."

[21] *Journal of Larocque from the Assiniboine to the Yellowstone*, 1805. Edited by L. J. Burpee in Publications of the Canadian Archives, no. 3, Ottawa, 1910.

[22] Davidson, *opus citra*, 82 n.

[23] For Thompson and Henry see Coues (E., ed.) *Manuscript Journal of Alexander Henry . . . and of David Thompson*, 3 vols., New York, 1897. Harmon (Daniel Williams) *Journal of Voyages and Travels in the Interior of North America*, Andover, N. H., 1820.

[24] Davidson, *opus citra*, 97.

[25] Coues, *opus citra*, 707 n.

In 1809 he again crossed the mountains and built Kullyspell House on the east shore of Lake Pend d'Oreille. From there he moved to the southeast up Clark's Fork of the Columbia and in November built the first Salish House[26] near the present site of Thompson Falls, Montana. It was not long after this that he or one of his companions built Spokane House and thus definitely entrenched the Northwest Company in the basin of the Columbia. After carrying his explorations down the Columbia to below the mouth of the Snake River Thompson claimed the whole country in the name of Great Britain.[27] In July, 1811, he reached the mouth of the Columbia.[28]

Ahead of Thompson, however, at the mouth of the Columbia was the first party of Astor's Pacific Fur Company under the command of Duncan McDougal and three others, all Scotchmen and formerly in the employ of the Northwest Company. McDougal received Thompson with cordiality and equipped him for the return journey. It was apparent to the Astorians that a fight with the Northwest Company was impending. Astor had sought the coöperation of this Company for his enterprise but his advances were rejected, and the struggle for the Columbia began.

The Pacific Fur Company was not content to sit down at Astoria and wait for furs to come. About the time Thompson appeared on the lower Columbia, David Stuart started for the interior to begin trade with the Indians. He selected a site about seven hundred miles up the river where he built Fort Okanagan.[29] In

[26] *Ibid.*, 606 n, 672 n, 674 n.

[27] Davidson, *opus citra*, 99.

[28] Cox (Ross) *Adventures on the Columbia River*, New York, 1832, 59.

[29] *Ibid.*, 84.

June, 1812, a second party was sent to the interior. Donald McKenzie led an expedition into the Nez Percé country and established a post on the Snake River.

The Northwesters had left a clerk named McMillan, a companion of Thompson's, in charge of Spokane House and he had two other posts under his command.[30] Of these Salish House about two hundred fifty miles northeast of Spokane was under the command of Finan McDonald. A Mr. Monteur had charge of the other post among the Kootenais probably near Kullyspell House about two hundred miles to the north. The American traders built a post near Spokane House. Cox and Farnham went to oppose McDonald among the Flatheads and Pillet led a small party into the Kootenai country. Both of these parties made a rich return of beavers.

The Northwest Company found its position strengthened by the War of 1812. Those of the Pacific Fur Company who were British subjects were unwilling to fight their countrymen and former associates and the threat of a British war vessel brought the surrender of the post. The merchandise of the Pacific Fur Company was sold to the Northwest Company for a sum much less than its value.[31] The affair appears to be tinged with an element of treachery.

With the fall of Astoria the dependent posts passed into the hands of the British fur traders. The Okana-

[30] "He (McMillan) had two other posts detached from this: one about two hundred and forty miles N. E. among a tribe called the Flatheads . . . other two hundred miles north among Cootinais in whose country there are plenty of beavers, deer, mountain sheep, and, at times, buffaloes." *Ibid.*, 100, 101.

[31] Text of Bill of Sale in Davidson, *opus citra*, Appendix M, 293.

gan post was continued, the Spokane post transferred to Spokane House, and the Nez Percé post moved to Fort Nez Percé near Walla Walla. Most of the Astor employes who were British subjects entered the employ of the Northwest Company. Among them were Ross Cox, John Read, Alexander Ross, and Duncan McDougall.

A large expedition was soon after sent into the interior to continue the trade. Read led a party into the Snake River country with which he had become acquainted while traveling overland to Astoria.[32] This party was destroyed by the Indians and the trade of that country for a time abandoned. Cox returned to the Flathead country where he was now to work with his old foe McMillan at Salish House, and at once began a lively trade.[33]

The Northwest Company did not depend entirely upon posts to sustain its trade. The Indians were inclined to be indolent, so large trapping expeditions under chosen leaders were sent to range the country for furs. Iroquois Indians were brought from the east in the hope that their example would encourage the western Indians to more activity in trapping.[34] The supervision of this interior trade was entrusted to Donald McKenzie who had been a partner in the Pacific Fur Company.[35] He was unpopular with the old Northwesters but was very successful in building up the western trade. He explored the country of the Snake

[32] Cox, *opus citra*, 115.
[33] *Ibid.*, 117.
[34] Ross (Alexander) *Fur Hunters of the Far West*, London, 1855, i, 74.
[35] *Ibid.*, 79.

River and even penetrated the region later known as Yellowstone Park.[36]

The Northwest Company had from the time of its formation been the rival of the Hudson's Bay Company who claimed a monopoly of the fur trade and was always ready to use its unlimited resources in killing off competitors. The Northwesters claimed to be successors of the old French traders and, like their famed predecessors, they cut heavily on the Hudson's Bay trade. The activities of the younger company forced the Hudson's Bay people to extend their posts westward. There was no one however with sufficient boldness to rival the explorations of Alexander Mackenzie[37] and David Thompson, but Hudson's Bay traders followed closely upon the heels of their competitors and demanded a share of all new trade. Among them was a Mr. Howes, who built Howes House near Flathead Lake in 1810.[38] In general, however, the Hudson's Bay Company limited its competition to the country east of the Rockies.[39] There the fight was carried on by violence and bloodshed, high prices for furs, and

[36] "Near the same lake (east of the Three Tetons) our people found a small rivulet of sulphurous water, bubbling out from the base of a perpendicular rock more than three hundred feet high. It was dark blue and tasted like gunpowder. Boiling fountains, having different degrees of temperature, were very numerous, one or two were so hot as to boil meat. In other parts, among the rocks, hot and cold springs might alternately be seen within a hundred yards of each other, differing in their temperature." *Ibid.*, i, 267.

[37] Mackenzie crossed the continent to the Pacific in 1793. Mackenzie (Alexander) *Voyages from Montreal through the Continent of North America to the frozen and Pacific Oceans* in 1789-1793, London, 1802.

[38] Ross, *opus citra*, ii, 9. Elliott (T. C.) *Columbia Fur Trade prior to 1811* in Washington Historical Society *Quarterly*, vi, No. 1, 9-10. Great Britain, *Columbia* (Coltman's Report) 1867, part ii, 92, states that Howes House was founded in 1810.

[39] McLeod (Malcolm) *Memorandum* in McLeod, *Journals*, 44, states that

the sale of vast quantities of rum to the Indians and with great financial loss to both sides. So serious did the losses finally become that both parties were willing to come to terms and in 1821 the two companies were united under the old name Hudson's Bay Company.[40]

The Hudson's Bay Company made few changes in the Columbia River trade. Dr. John McLoughlin, a native of Canada, of mixed French and Irish descent, and an old Northwester was made chief factor, and given supervision of the trade of this region. He was a man of surpassing ability. He had wonderful powers of command and was a remarkable judge of men. His temper was violent but he was tolerant and kindly of disposition, and showed strong friendship for Americans who came into his country.[41]

McLoughlin did not think the company headquarters at Fort George (Astoria) were suitable and he founded Fort Vancouver on the north bank of the Columbia where he took up his residence. It was from here that he despatched his brigades of trappers and traders and it was from here that he shipped immense cargoes of furs to Asia and Europe. McLoughlin had under his command an array of brilliant traders, who in their efforts to supply the demand for beaver hats, have made so fascinating the history of the fur trade in the Northwest. Among them were Peter Skene Ogden, James McMillan, James Douglas, and Alexander Ross, old associates of McLoughlin in the Northwest Company. In addition there were Alexander R. Mc-

the Hudson's Bay Company had no trade west of the Rockies until after its coalition with the Northwest Company in 1821.

40 Davidson, *opus citra*, chapter vii.

41 Fitzgerald, *An Examination of the Charter and Proceedings of the Hudson's Bay Company. . .* London, 1849, 13.

Leod, James W. Dease, Archibald McDonald, Donald Ross, Francis and Edward Ermatinger, and John Work,[42] all of whom were at some time to distinguish themselves.

Alexander Ross was intrusted with the Snake River trade, and placed in command of a large body of traders and trappers, many of whom were Indians. He started from Spokane and went up Clark's Fork to Salish House. From there he went up the Flathead River to some place south of Flathead Lake. Thence he marched directly for Hell's Gate (Missoula, Montana) and camped where Work was to camp eight years later.[43] From here he went up the Bitter Root to Ross's Hole and spent the winter trading with the Flatheads. In the spring of 1824 he traveled through the mountains to the source of Clark's Fork near Butte, Montana, and crossed the main ridge of the Rockies to the headwaters of the Missouri. He returned to Salish House in November with five thousand beaver and many other pelts. This expedition was exceptionally profitable to the Company.[44]

After this successful expedition Ross was given command of Salish House (the Flathead post) and Ogden as chief trader, was sent to lead the brigade during the winter of 1824-1825. Ogden was as successful as Ross had been and reported a "country richer in beaver than

---

42 Hudson's Bay Company *Council Minutes* 1825, in McLeod, *Journals*, 21. Ogden and McLeod left interesting journals. Archibald McDonald left a number of valuable letters. Copies of these are in the Canadian Archives. Alexander Ross wrote two books regarding his experiences.

43 October 20, 1831.

44 Ross, *opus citra*, ii, 8-140. Ross wrote that this was "the most profitable ever brought from the Snake River in one year." *Ibid.*, 140. See also Governor Simpson to John McLeod, November 1, 1824, in McLeod, *Journals*, 12.

any they had ever seen." [45] So promising did this field appear that additional men were sent to help carry on the trade, among them John Work and James W. Dease. The latter was given charge of the Flathead post where he remained during the winter of 1826-1827.[46] Ogden remained in general control of the whole interior trade until 1831.[47] During this time he commanded brigades that traded in the region of Great Salt Lake and Ogden's Hole, and even down into California, besides exploring the whole region of the headwaters of the Snake and Columbia. Ogden was succeeded in command of the Snake River brigade by John Work, who traded in the interior as far as the headwaters of the Missouri, to Ogden's River and the Great Salt Lake, and also into California. He extended his travels beyond the limits of Ogden's expeditions. In 1834 he was transferred to the trade on the Northwest coast.[48]

After 1827 the beaver trade in the Northwest began to decrease.[49] This was due in part to the heavy slaugh-

45 McLoughlin to Governor Simpson, Fort Vancouver, August 8, 1826. *Ibid.*, 69.

46 William Kitson to John McLeod, Kootenai House, March 8, 1827. *Ibid.*, 93.

47 Elliott (T. C.) *Columbia Fur Trade*, 23. Morice (A. G.) *Northern Interior of British Columbia*, Toronto, 1904, 168.

48 John Work to Edward Ermatinger, Columbia River, December 13, 1834. *Papers, re British Columbia* in Canadian Archives.

49 "Mr. Dease has taken the Flathead post in charge for the winter and to his sorrow will not turn out more than one-third of its last year's return." William Kitson to John McLeod, Kootenai House, March 8, 1827. McLeod *Journals*, 93. ". . . the Indian trade at the Flatheads is declining;" John Work to J. McLeod. Colville, March 25, 1828. *Ibid.*, 110. George Keith wrote to J. McLeod, April 16, 1829, that the Columbia trade "appears to be declining." *Ibid.*, 119. Angus Bethume wrote to McLeod, March 30, 1830. "Columbia still going down hill, and will continue to go rapidly, I think." *Ibid.*, 127.

ter of beaver by Indian and white trappers but probably more to the growing competition of the Americans.

The Americans developed the fur trade on the upper Missouri and carried it into the Rockies largely by individual effort and without the efficient organization that characterized the British fur trading companies. The trade along the Missouri began before the close of the eighteenth century, with headquarters at St. Louis.[50] The most prominent of the early St. Louis traders were the Spaniard, Manuel Lisa, and the Frenchmen, Auguste and Pierre Chouteau. They shipped their furs to Montreal where they were purchased by the Northwest Company. John Jacob Astor tried to open up a trade with them as early as 1800 but without success.[51]

After the British were barred from American territory Manuel Lisa was the first to establish a trade on the upper Missouri. Soon after the Lewis and Clark expedition he led a party up the Missouri to the mouth of the Yellowstone, thence up that river to the mouth of the Bighorn where he established a trading post. This post was in the heart of the Crow country and rich

[50] Missouri Historical Society, *Collections*, iv, 9, gives an account of the organization in 1794 of *The Commercial Company for the Discovery of Nations of the Upper Missouri.* One Jacques Clamorgan appears as the most active promoter. The Company obtained from Spain a monopoly of the fur trade of the upper Missouri. The Auguste Chouteau, *Papers*, in the Missouri Historical Library contain references to the Missouri fur trade as early as 1795.

[51] "Je regrette beaucoup de n'avoir jamais pu realizer le désire dont Je me suis flatté il y a long temps, de visiter votre pays, pour y establir des liaisons de Commerce. . . Ne sera-t-il pas possible pour vous d'en envoyer tout droit de votre pays jusqu'ici? Je ne doute pas que cela ne puisse faire, et même à notre avantage mutuel – dans un tel cas, il ne me seroit plus necessaire d'aller à Montreal dont je vous assure je serois bien rejoui: car non seulement les frais de voyage, mais se que vous encore plus, la perte de trois mois de temps, seraient ainsi evites." John Jacob Astor to Auguste Chouteau, New York, January 28, 1800. Pierre Chouteau, *Collections*.

in beaver. The Crows were enemies of the Blackfeet and apparently were glad to welcome the Americans. The Blackfeet had long traded with the British and, apparently incited by their white friends, they began an open hostility towards the Americans which continued for many years. Lisa soon returned to St. Louis and his post was abandoned,[52] but the trade on the upper Missouri was not allowed to die.

Manuel Lisa was so impressed with the possibilities of the fur trade on the upper Missouri that he decided to form a company of the leading fur traders of St. Louis to carry it on. He joined with Pierre and Auguste Chouteau, William Clark, and five others to found the Missouri Fur Company which was incorporated in 1808.[53] Apparently Astor sought to join but was refused. In June of the following year Lisa obtained from Governor Meriwether Lewis a license giving him and his associates the exclusive right to trade on the upper Missouri.[54]

The first expedition of the new company under Lisa's command started up the Missouri in the summer of 1809. The party was large and well equipped both for trapping and fighting the Indians. Lisa spent the winter at his old post near the mouth of the Bighorn, where apparently a large number of beaver pelts were traded from the Crows. The following spring two of the partners, Pierre Menard and Andrew Henry crossed

[52] This post was sometimes called Fort Manuel and sometimes Fort Lisa. Chittenden (Hiram) *History of the American Fur Trade in the Far West*, New York, 1902, i, 126.

[53] *Articles d'association et de societé fait et conclu par et entre Benjamen Wilkinsen, Pierre Chouteau pere, Manul Lisa, Auguste Chouteau jeune . . . dans les vues de traiter et chasser dans le haut du Missoury. . .* Pierre Chouteau, *Collections*.

[54] *Lisa Papers.* Envelope, i, 7, June, 1809, in Missouri Historical Library.

over the divide which separates the Yellowstone from the Gallatin River and built a post where the three forks of the Missouri unite. Here was a rich beaver country and trade was lively. The Blackfoot Indians, however, did not accept the Americans and began a series of attacks upon them. They stole their horses, their traps, their furs, and made it unsafe for any of the party to venture out of the post. So dangerous did the hostility of the Blackfeet become that Henry abandoned the post and crossed over the mountains to one of the tributaries of the Snake River, ever since then known as Henry's Fork.[55]

Misfortunes continued to follow the activities of the Missouri Fur Company. Fire destroyed a vast store of furs and impoverished the Company. The competition of Astor's Pacific Fur Company looked dangerous. The hostility of the Blackfeet continued to hinder trade on the upper Missouri. The War of 1812 stopped the export of beaver and forced a sharp drop in prices.[56] The Company continually declined although it underwent several reorganizations with Lisa's influence continually growing. One by one the other partners dropped out and some of them formed competing companies.

After Lisa's death in 1820 the Missouri Fur Company regained some of its former vigor.[57] It established

[55] Dale (H. C.) *The Ashley-Smith Explorations and the Discovery of a Central Route to the Pacific*, Cleveland, 1918, 30-31, quotes James, *Three Years among the Indians and Mexicans*, Waterloo, Illinois, 1846, 10-32. James accompanied this expedition.

[56] Cavalier, a merchant of St. Louis, wrote Auguste Chouteau from New Orleans, March 1, 1809, ". . . nous voyons que l'ambargo, vous a empeché de nous faire de remiter sur les quelles nous comptionne vous avez tres bien priver que d'apres cette mesure la pelletemic Seroit sans voleuir. Auguste Chouteau, *Papers*.

a new post at the mouth of the Bighorn and named it Fort Benton[58] for Senator Benton the distinguished representative of the fur trading interests in Congress. In 1823 a large party under Jones and Immil set out from this fort to open trade with the long hostile Blackfeet. Many packs of beaver were collected but when the expedition seemed assured of success it was attacked by the Blackfeet, most of the men killed and all the furs and equipment stolen. This blow practically ended the operations of the Missouri Fur Company in the Northwest. It continued to trade in other territories for some years under the leadership of Joshua Pilcher, who in 1828 made one last effort to recover the trade of the far Northwest. In July of that year he left Green River and proceeded towards the Northwest. He crossed the Beaverhead country and spent the winter on Flathead Lake. In the spring he continued his journey to Fort Colville. From there he went east with a party belonging to the Hudson's Bay Company. He found this company so strong in the mountains that he made no effort to open up trade in that region, and henceforth the Missouri Fur Company ceased to be of much significance.

Of far more importance than the Missouri Fur Company was John Jacob Astor's American Fur Company. This concern was chartered in 1808 and carried on a fur trade in all parts of America. Astor was interested in the trade of the far Northwest and as has already been told sought to establish his influence there by means of the Pacific Fur Company. When this failed Astor turned his attention to the Mis-

[57] Chittenden, *opus citra*, i, 150 n.

[58] Not to be confused with the later Fort Benton on the Missouri.

souri River trade. He had to fight a number of St. Louis traders, notably the Missouri Fur Company, Stone and Company, and the powerful Chouteau interests. In 1822 the American Fur Company established a western department with headquarters at St. Louis. Stone and Company was soon united with this new venture and a little later the directions of this department was intrusted to Bernard Pratte, the father-in-law of Ramsey Crooks who was one of Astor's ablest lieutenants. Pratte soon formed a connection with Pierre Chouteau under the name of Pratte, Chouteau and Company. This firm managed the western department until 1838 when after the death of Bernard Pratte and the retirement of Pierre Chouteau the management of the business passed into the hands of Pierre Chouteau Jr., who operated under the firm name of Pierre Chouteau Jr., and Company.[59]

In the meantime the American Fur Company strengthened its hold on the upper Missouri by buying out a small but energetic and ambitious rival the so-called Columbia Fur Company. This occurred in 1827 and henceforth the organizations of the Columbia Fur Company passed under the designation of the Upper Missouri outfit.

With the elimination of all rivals for the Missouri River trade the American Fur Company began a definite program of pushing up the river. Its first step was the construction of a fort near the junction of the Missouri and Yellowstone Rivers, a post which later was known as Fort Union. The leader of this undertaking was Kenneth McKenzie and he soon attempted to open

[59] Chittenden, *opus citra*, i, 127-157 gives history of Missouri Fur Company.

a trade with the Blackfeet. In the fall of 1830 he sent an expedition to the Blackfoot country. The party went up the Missouri to the mouth of the Marias and then marched up that river for some distance when the Blackfeet were encountered. This time through the mediation of an old trader who knew them well, friendship was promised and American trade with the Blackfeet began. The next year in 1831 McKenzie sent another party under James Kipp to establish a post among the Blackfeet. It was in October of that year about the time that John Work was trailing through Lolo Pass or up the Blackfoot valley that Kipp began the construction of Piegan Post at the mouth of the Marias River. Kipp with a bountiful supply of alcohol carried on a prosperous trade with the Indians for a year and then returned to Fort Union. His fort was soon after burned by the Indians but the next year Fort McKenzie a few miles farther up the river was built to take its place. This placc long remained the headquarters for American trade with the Blackfeet.

In the same year McKenzie established Fort Cass at the mouth of the Bighorn as a center for trade with the Crow Indians. Fort McKenzie and Fort Cass dominated the Indian trade on the upper Missouri and the Yellowstone for a decade. About 1843 Fort McKenzie was abandoned in favor of Fort Chardon at the mouth of the Judith. This location was not favorable however and the headquarters for the Blackfoot trade was moved up the Missouri about eighteen miles above the present Fort Benton and Fort Lewis erected in the new location. This location did not prove suitable and in 1846 Fort Lewis was moved down the river and a new post established which in 1850 was renamed Fort

Benton in honor of the vigorous champion of the fur trade, then United States senator from Missouri. On the Yellowstone, Fort Cass had as tributaries Fort Van Buren near the mouth of the Tongue River built in 1835, Fort Alexander opposite the mouth of the Rosebud built in 1839, and Fort Sarpy about twenty-five miles below Fort Cass, built about 1843.[60]

The Rocky Mountain Fur Company and the companies that grew out of it constituted the most serious threat to the supremacy of the American Fur Company in the northwest. The founder, and for some years the dominant figure in this concern, was William Henry Ashley.[61] He brought to his service a number of brilliant men without whose efforts and ability the success of the new trading company would have been impossible. First of all was Andrew Henry[62] of the old Missouri Fur Company. After many misfortunes he was to fall upon a rich beaver country only to retire when wealth was almost within sight. There was Jedediah S. Smith[63] who gained his first experience in the employ of Ashley and who added much to the world's knowledge of western geography. Among the other distinguished members of this company were Milton and William Sublette, Thomas Fitzpatrick, Robert Campbell, Henry Fraeb, and the famous trapper and explorer, James Bridger.[64]

Ashley planned to begin operations on the upper Missouri in the territory that for more than a decade

---

60 See *ibid.*, 309-395 for good sketch of the American Fur Company's operations in the west.

61 For life of Ashley, see Dale, *opus citra*, part ii.

62 *Ibid.*, 63, see also *supra.*

63 *Ibid.*, part iii.

64 Chittenden, *opus citra*, i, chapter xv.

had been worked by the Missouri Fur Company and smaller concerns. Instead of building posts, however, he thought to get the beaver by sending out parties to trap them. When the trapping season was over all the trappers in Henry's employ and all other trappers whether Indian or white who desired to trade with him would gather at an appointed place known as the rendezvous.[65] Thus he was imitating the policy inaugurated in the Northwest by the Northwest Company's Snake River brigades. The Northwest Company, however, had posts instead of the rendezvous.

Andrew Henry set out for the Yellowstone with the first expedition in 1822, and the next spring was followed by Ashley with a second party. The hostility of the Indians, however, caused both expeditions to end in failure.

During the fall of 1823 Thomas Fitzpatrick discovered South Pass an easy entrance into the valley of Green River, a region rich in beaver. Into this country in the spring of 1824 went Henry to begin a trade that was to make many fortunes. Henry soon retired leaving Smith, Sublette, and Etienne Provost in charge of the expedition. Smith led his party during the summer of 1824 across the mountains to Snake River, and from there across to the Clark's Fork of the Columbia. Here he fell in with a band of Iroquois detached from the brigade under command of Alexander Ross from whom he obtained all their furs, and accompanied them to Ross's headquarters apparently with the intention of getting some further profits.[66] Ross was at the junction of Pahsiman Creek and Salmon River in the

[65] Dale, *opus citra*, 67.

[66] *Ibid.*, 97, Ross, *opus citra*, ii, 127.

present state of Idaho, and from there Smith accompanied him over the divide into Ross's Hole then down the Bitter Root to Salish House where he was to meet Peter Skene Ogden who had been given charge of the Snake River brigades. The next spring Smith returned to Green River probably in company with Ogden's brigade.

Another party under the command of Provost explored the interior and discovered the Great Salt Lake. Sublette and Smith joined Provost in this neighborhood some time during the summer of 1825 and succeeded in getting a number of Ogden's men to desert and bring with them a quantity of furs.[67]

In the summer of 1825 Ashley arrived at Green River to conduct his first great rendezvous. He had come up the Platte River to its forks, then followed the South Platte far into Colorado, then going northwest had crossed the divide by Bridger's Pass.[68] So successful had been Ashley's trappers and so large had been the trade with Indians and free trappers that after this summer's trade Ashley was enabled to retire a rich man.[69]

Ashley was succeeded by the firm of Smith, Jackson, and Sublette. The company still had a virtual monopoly of a rich beaver country save for the occasional visits of a Hudson's Bay Company brigade, but the new leaders resolved to expand their business west of Great Salt Lake and possibly to find an outlet to the Pacific.

[67] T. C. Elliott states this from John Work's *Journal* in his *Peter Skene Ogden, Fur Trader*, Oregon Historical Society *Quarterly*, xi, 20. See also Dale, 107. Chittenden states the value of these furs was from seventy to two hundred thousand dollars, i, 277.

[68] Dale, *opus citra*, 116, 123-133.

[69] *Ibid.*, 168 n.

Smith led the first expedition westward starting in August, 1826. He traveled in a southwestward direction until he struck the line of the later Santa Fe Railroad which he followed into California. He found few furs but encountered many hardships. He left most of his men in California and returned to the rendezvous in the summer of 1827. He remained there only a month and started back to California with a force of nineteen men. He arrived there short of provisions and found his men in a like condition with himself. The Spaniards were suspicious and anxious to get the Americans out of the country. Smith signed an agreement to leave the country and was allowed to purchase supplies. He started east during the winter by a new route and in April, 1828, found his road blocked by high mountains.[70]

Smith then turned towards the northwest and after reaching the coast followed it northward. The road was difficult but the Indians gave no cause for alarm. As the party approached the Willamette valley on the thirteenth of July it met the Umpqua Indians who also seemed friendly. The next morning, however, the Indians attacked the Americans and killed all except Smith and two others, who escaped to Fort Vancouver. McLoughlin at once sent an expedition to punish the Indians and recover the stolen property. Much of it was retaken and McLoughlin paid Smith about twenty thousand dollars for his furs.[71]

[70] *Ibid.*, 237 n.

[71] Chittenden, *opus citra*, i, 286. "August W. Smith an American left [ ] California with three hundred and fifteen mules. In July party destroyed at Umpqua. Mr. McLeod sent party to retake property. Move unpopular." *Journal of John Stuart at Rocky Mountain House*, July 15, 1829. This surely refers to J. S. Smith.

Smith spent the winter at Fort Vancouver as the guest of McLoughlin and the next spring went with a Hudson's Bay brigade up the Columbia and across to Salish House from where he returned to the rendezvous.[72] He found his partners had not been successful in their hunts. The winter had been very severe; many men were lost, and the Indians would not furnish supplies, owing, it was suspected, to the influence of Ogden.

It appears that Smith, in return for the help he had received from McLoughlin, had promised to abandon the Snake River country. He accordingly induced his partners to cross the mountains into the old beaver country around the Yellowstone and Madison Rivers. Here they encountered once more their old enemies the Blackfeet, and they met also a more determined enemy in the American Fur Company. The rendezvous of 1830 on the Wind River was the last conducted by Smith, Sublette, and Bridger, but it brought large profits.

After this rendezvous, Smith, Jackson, and Sublette sold their business to a group of younger men who continued the Rocky Mountain Fur Company. The most important members of this group were Milton Sublette, Thomas Fitzpatrick, James Bridger, and Henry Fraeb. These men started a vigorous trade with all the Indians of the Rocky Mountain Northwest. The American Fur Company was determined to share this trade and sent parties to follow its competitors. The next two years were full of rivalry between these two concerns. In 1831 American Fur Company traders followed Fraeb and Fitzpatrick who were trading in the Powder River country. These two latter, however, ran away

[72] Dale, *opus citra*, 277, n.

from their rivals and spent the winter trading with the Indians west of the divide. Work possibly had this party in mind in his entry of December 16, 1831. The American Fur Company traders continued to follow and the Rocky Mountain traders sought to escape. The latter traveled over the country drained by the headwaters of the Snake River and into Pierre's Hole but the American Fur Company brigade was always by their side. The rendezvous for 1832 was at Pierre's Hole. Here were gathered the bands of the Rocky Mountain Fur Company and a party of the American Fur Company, besides a number of free trappers. Here came also Nathaniel Wyeth from Boston and Captain Bonneville. Among those present at this rendezvous were doubtless some of the Americans whom John Work mentions as invading his country.

The Rocky Mountain Fur Company was putting up a losing battle with its great rival. It could not stand the fierce competition and in 1834 held its last great rendezvous. Shortly after this Fitzpatrick, Sublette, and Bridger entered the service of the American Fur Company which thenceforth dominated the fur trade throughout all the Northwest east of the continental divide.

The region now known as Montana and Idaho early became the battle ground of the rival British and American fur traders. The fall of Astoria and the failure of the Pacific Fur Company merely delayed the struggle until the Americans could creep up upon the British by way of the Missouri or over the Oregon Trail. Since the British had established their trade in this country after the War of 1812, they sought only to maintain their monopoly while the Americans were the aggressors. Ross states the situation with precision as follows:

> Our southern and more enterprising neighbors have not lost sight of the advantages offered them, but continue year after year advancing with hasty strides, scouring the country and carrying off the cream of the trade; and if we do not speedily bestir ourselves the Yankee will reap all the advantages of our discoveries.[73]

The methods of competition were unscrupulous and frequently violent. Alcohol was used in large quantities to seduce the Indian to sell his furs. Astor had forbidden the Pacific Fur Company traders to sell or give intoxicating drink to the Indians[74] but it is doubtful if they obeyed his orders. The Northwest Company early found that the liberal use of rum was effective with the Indians and their traders used it unsparingly when there were competitors near their field.[75] The Hudson's Bay Company forbade the use of alcohol in the Indian trade but apparently there was no expectation that these orders would be obeyed. When competition arose there was no hesitancy in resorting to alcohol to hold or win the Indians.[76]

[73] *Fur Hunters*, ii, 143.

[74] *Ibid.*, i, 15.

[75] John Dunn, a Hudson's Bay Company trader and hostile to the Northwest Company, declared that this Company ruined the Indian with spirits. *The Oregon Territory and the British North American Fur Trade*, Philadelphia, 1845, 28. Morice, *opus citra*, 113, declares that the Northwest Company introduced rum into the Northwest.

[76] In 1831 the Hudson's Bay Company forbade the sale of rum to the Indians. *Ibid.*, 114. This of course did not prevent the gift of rum. Governor Simpson testified before a committee of the House of Commons in 1857 that rum was never sold to the Indians except some on the frontier. He admitted that use of spirits was great during the fight with the Americans. Great Britain, House of Commons, *Report of Committee on Hudson's Bay Company*, 31 July, 1857, 58-61. At the same hearing John McLoughlin testified that the Americans restricted the use of alcohol and that the Hudson's Bay Company used it excessively. *Ibid.*, 284. I cannot learn whether

The United States Government from time to time issued stringent prohibitions against the sale of rum to the Indians. It was to check the evil of alcohol among the Indians that it maintained the system of licenses, and those who were caught debauching the natives were generally deprived of their right to trade.[77] In spite of all the efforts of the government, however, great quantities of liquor were smuggled into the Indian country.[78] These free traders and even the American Fur Company justified its use on the ground that it was used by the Hudson's Bay Company.

The fur traders all knew the demoralizing effect of alcohol upon the Indian. Every day of drunkenness robbed him of a day's hunt and made him less efficient when in the woods. The use of alcohol was most extensive in the third and fourth decade of the century. It so seriously affected the Indian trade that the fur companies came to depend more and more upon white trappers or upon Indians trapping under the direction of white leaders.[79]

There are many instances of sharp practices recorded in the Indian trade. In 1822 a body of Americans induced a number of Iroquois to desert the Hudson's

---

or not this was Dr. John McLoughlin but the testimony appears to be in agreement with his feeling. Great Britain, House of Commons, *Report from Select Committee on Aborigines*, 1837, tells much of use of liquor in securing Indian trade.

[77] Chittenden, *opus citra*, chapter iv.

[78] McLean, a Hudson's Bay trader, wrote: "In the course of the winter (1822) a Yankee adventurer opened a 'grog' shop within a short distance of the depot." When an Indian, who had been equipped by McLean, returned in March with his hunt he began trading his furs for "grog." McLean then seized the furs, and paid the balance due the Indian in rum. *Twenty-five Years Service in Hudson's Bay Company*, London, 1849, i, 61, 62.

[79] Great Britain, House of Commons, *Report from Select Committee on Hudson's Bay Company*, 1857.

Bay Company's brigade and work for them. Ross recounts how in 1823 he allowed a party of Iroquois to hunt by themselves. After a time they returned "trapless and beaverless; naked and destitute of almost everything; and in debt to the American trappers for having conveyed them to the Trois Tetons." Old Pierre, their leader, told of two months of successful trapping when the Snakes stole everything. The Iroquois fell in with some Americans whom they promised forty dollars to escort them to the main party. The Americans' story did not fully agree with Old Pierre's and Ross learned that the former had already obtained more than a hundred beaver skins from the Iroquois. Ross finally came to believe his Indians had not been robbed but while hunting had fallen in with the Americans who succeeded in seducing them "to their side under the pretext of giving them five dollars for every beaver skin they might deliver at the Yellowstone River where the Americans had a trading post, that with the view of profit by this contemplated speculation, they had left their furs *en cache* with those of the American party where they had been hunting, and had come back, not with the intention of remaining with us, but rather . . . to get what they could from us, and then to seduce their comrades to desert in a body with their furs to the Americans." [80]

The Hudson's Bay people showed no higher standards of conduct than did the Americans. In a letter written in 1839 is an account of an effort to capture a

[80] Ross, *Fur Hunters*, ii, 129. This was Jedediah Smith, the most devout and religious of all the fur traders. Dale, *opus citra*, 96, puts a somewhat better light on Smith's actions.

British subject who was trading for the Americans among "our Piegans."[81]

McLoughlin found the most effective way of meeting American competition was by cutting the price of merchandise and paying a high price for furs. He claimed, however, that even after radically changing prices he could still make a fair profit, while the Americans were sure to lose.[82] McLoughlin, however, sometimes became quite indignant at the efforts of the Americans. Referring probably to Nathaniel Wyeth or Captain Bonneville, he wrote in 1833; "But it is galling to think that a bankrupt Yankee unacquainted with the business should have been able to oblige us to pay so dear."[83]

Bonneville soon gave up the fur trade and returned to the army. Wyeth who built Fort Hall in 1832 found himself fighting a powerful and relentless monopoly. McLoughlin not only cut prices so as to deprive Wyeth of all chance of profit, but he built a post just west of Fort Hall and notified all the Indians that if they traded with the Americans he would not trade with them. As a result Wyeth was soon compelled to sell out to the Hudson's Bay Company[84] and return to Boston.

[81] John Rowand Edmonton, January 5, 1839, in *Letters of Donald Ross*, in Canadian Archives.

[82] "I broke up the American party in the Snake country and I did this simply by underselling them and showing them we could afford to sell the trappers at European servants' prices and give them ten per made beaver and clear handsomely by them." McLoughlin, Fort Vancouver, February 1, 1830, in McLeod, *Journals*, 123.

[83] Fort Vancouver, March 1, 1833, *ibid.*, 173.

[84] Dunn says that Wyeth "tried a fur trading speculation and failed, from want of skill, or capital, or liberality of dealing. The company purchased this post from him on liberal terms, almost a gratuity." *Opus citra*, 222.

In the Flathead country vigorous measures were adopted to overcome American aggressiveness. John Work in 1826 hurried three boats loaded with merchandise up the river to the Flatheads when he heard that Americans were approaching. Some time before this Dease had recommended that Kootenai Post be abandoned. The American peril, however, led him to reconsider this plan and he urged that both the post and the Flathead post be strengthened.[85] This recommendation was followed although the Flathead post was moved farther east to ward off the Americans.[86] A few years later it was moved again to Post Creek near the site of the present St. Ignatius, Montana, and named Fort Connah. Construction was started by McArthur and completed by Angus McDonald in 1847.[87] This was the last Hudson's Bay post to be constructed within the present limits of the United States.

In 1833 the American Fur Company and the Hudson's Bay Company made an agreement defining the limits of each one's activities.[88] The next year when the Rocky Mountain Fur Company came to an end there was a prospect for peace in the fur country. American adventurers, however, still made invasions of the lands west of the mountains and forced a liberal treatment of Indian and white trappers.[89]

85 October 15, 1826, *ibid.*, 73.

86 John Work to Edward Ermatinger. Flatheads, March 19, 1830.

87 Bancroft (H. H.) *Works*, xxviii (*Northwest Coast* ii), 74. See also, Angus McDonald, *A Few Items of the West*, 1889.

88 R. Crooks writes, June 26, 1837, that he was considering renewal of this agreement made March 21, 1833. American Fur Company, *Letters*, no. 5, in New York Historical Library.

89 "The trade . . . is on a more liberal scale than in early days in the Columbia, especially in the upper country both with Indians and freemen, in consequence of the number of new adventures now pouring in upon us from

Although the Hudson's Bay Company was able to drive out American fur traders from the Columbia basin it was to fall before a new American invasion. Missionaries came to convert the Indians and they were followed by large numbers of settlers who proposed to occupy the land.[90] Their efforts led to destruction of the game and furthered the decline of the fur trade. The treaty of 1846 put an end to the Hudson's Bay Company's control of the fur trade of the Northwest.

The beaver of the Northwest were of good quality[91] and the supply was large. The number of pelts grew steadily until in 1837 it amounted to twenty-six thousand seven hundred and thirty-five. The total importations of beaver from all the Hudson's Bay Company domains in 1834 was fifty-seven thousand three hundred and ninety-three pelts of which about twenty-one thousand came from the Columbia River country.[92] After 1837 the Hudson's Bay Company's supply of beaver from the Columbia declined until in 1845 it amounted to seventeen thousand two hundred and ninety pelts and in 1848 to only twelve thousand seven hundred and fif-

the American side of the mountains." Archibald McDonald to McLoughlin. Colville, January 25, 1837, McLeod, *Journals*, 191.

90 "The traversing of the continent (from Missouri River to Columbia) is now becoming more safe and familiar to our ear every day. I have now St. Louis cows and horses at Colville – two or three American clergymen with their families, and household goods came across last season. . . . We must now absolutely make a bold stand on the frontiers." Archibald McDonald to J. McLeod, Colville, January 25, 1837. *Ibid.*, 191.

91 "From the northwest coast there is imported into Boston every year a considerable collection of furs. The beaver from there is generally dark, fine pelted, and good seasoned, at present worth in this market an average of about twenty shillings per pound." American Fur Company, *Catalogue. General Observations as to the Present Value and Prospects for Furs*, London, December 21, 1837.

92 C. M. Lampson to R. Crooks. London, May 13, 1837. American Fur Company *Letters.*

ty-six pelts.[93] The trade east of the Rockies cannot be stated so definitely but in general it followed the rise and decline of the trade in the Columbia basin. This decline in production was accompanied by a decreased demand for beaver. Silk hats and hats of nutria had succeeded beaver in public favor.

The price of beaver generally advanced from the beginning of the century until about 1840. In 1800 beaver were sold at St. Louis at one dollar a pound, amounting to about one dollar and twenty-five cents for a pelt. In 1809 the price had increased to two dollars a pound,[94] and rose quickly to four dollars, but due to the War of 1812 soon dropped to two dollars and fifty cents where it stayed till 1815.[95] Thereafter it rose steadily until in 1834 Kenneth McKenzie paid more than four dollars at Fort Union[96] which was considerably below the St. Louis price. After 1840 the price declined until in 1848 the Hudson's Bay Company paid only one dollar at Fort Vancouver for a large skin.[97] The market rapidly recovered however, and in 1850 was about a dollar and fifty cents at Fort Vancouver, and in 1851 was two dollars and fifty cents. There was hope that the old prices would come back but the great demand for beaver was forever gone.[98]

The Hudson's Bay Company obtained other important furs from the Northwest. In 1835 it obtained thir-

93 American Fur Company, *Memorandum.* 1845 and 1848.

94 Auguste Chouteau *Collections.*

95 *Ibid.*, Chittenden, *opus citra*, i, 145 n.

96 Pierre Chouteau *Collections.*

97 James Douglas to F. Tolmie, May 14, 1848. *Fort Nisqually Letter Book*, 52.

98 "The price of beaver is gradually on the rise and maintains itself as formerly in the market as almost to inspire hopes of a return of better times." James Douglas to F. Tolmie, April 21, 1851. *Papers re British Columbia* in Canadian Archives.

ty thousand muskrats, six thousand five hundred martens, two thousand five hundred otters, two thousand five hundred mink, besides bear, fishers, lynx, and silver, cross, and red foxes.[99]

The trade in buffalo robes was limited to the country east of the mountains and was slow to develop. Europe did not care for them and the demand in America had to be created. The papers of the American Fur Company contain many discussions of the way to create a market. The Americans developed a demand for them as overcoats and as robes for sleighs and carriages, and after 1825 the market was fairly steady at the price of about four dollars and fifty cents for each first class robe.[100]

It is difficult to determine the actual number of buffalo robes that were brought to market from the upper Missouri. In 1839 Pierre Chouteau estimated that Fort Union had collected twenty-four thousand and the Sioux posts thirty-two thousand robes.[101] This, however, left unaccounted for a large number gathered from independent sources. In 1839, moreover, the trade in buffalo robes had been declining for a period of ten years. Probably this decline was due to the fact

[99] American Fur Company, *Memorandum, 1835.*

[100] Chittenden, *opus citra*, ii, 817. The American Fur Company's price list from 1820 to 1840 gives about the same price each year for buffalo robes.

[101] American Fur Company *Letters.* July 18, 1839. G[eorge] E.[hninger] to Ramsey Crooks. Fort Clark, a small post in the Mandan country, furnished one hundred and eighty-eight packs of ten robes per pack in 1833. Alexander Kennedy, *Journal of Occurrences at Fort Clark* in Pierre Chouteau, *Collections.* The American Fur Company estimated that in 1841 there were sold twenty-six thousand six hundred and eighty-one buffalo robes and six thousand eight hundred and eleven calves at a total price of one hundred and twenty-nine thousand dollars. *General Abstract of Sales of Buffalo Robes*, 1841. James Hall, a statistical writer, stated that there were shipped through New Orleans thirteen thousand four hundred and twelve packs of buffalo robes in 1827, nineteen thousand nine hundred

that during the thirties furs were not in high favor among the "society" people.

In the fur country the only currency was the beaver pelt. All other pelts and all merchandise was valued in terms of beaver. In spite of the variations in the supply of furs the ratio of beaver to other skins remained practically fixed because of the prejudice of the Indian against change. For this reason the price of furs in terms of beaver in the Indian country was quite different from the price at the great fur markets.[102]

The net profits from the fur trade varied greatly with the ability and luck of the trader and with the condition of the market. Before 1800 the Hudson's Bay Company often made a profit of sixty per cent. This was before competition seriously affected the trade. During the fight with the Northwest Company there were often no dividends. After 1821 the company regularly paid five per cent with an annual bonus

and eighty-seven packs in 1828, thirteen thousand two hundred and ten packs in 1829, three thousand sixty-one packs in 1830 and two thousand five hundred and fifty-four packs in 1831. *Statistics of the West at the Close of the Year* 1836, Cincinnati, 1836, 207. After the first quarter of the century woolen coats and robes began to supplant the buffalo. The price remained about the same but the number put on the market decreased.

102 In 1850 a gun costing originally two shillings would sell for twenty beaver worth thirty-two pounds and ten shillings, or sixty marten worth forty-six pounds and ten shillings, or twenty otter worth twenty pounds. Coltman's *Report*, 20.

103 Great Britain, Colonial Office. *Return to Address of Parliament*, May 20, 1842. A defence of the Hudson's Bay Company. "Up to this period H. B. C. had no cause to complain of interference with inland trade. . . But rights of territory and trade invaded by rival traders at this time caused feuds, loss of life, destruction of property, breach of peace, etc., which were injurious to natives because they brought unrestricted use of liquor, so that Indians', between 1800 and 1821, dividends for first eight years were only four per cent, during next six years no dividend, for last

of six to ten per cent until 1841,[103] making an average return of about twelve per cent.[104]

McLoughlin estimated that the Columbia department cleared nearly thirty-two thousand pounds sterling in 1828 and 1829 at a time when American competition was keen.[105] By 1833 the Columbia trade was declining and the profits were only twenty thousand pounds. One writer states that a quantity of furs purchased at Vancouver for six hundred and sixty pounds sold in London for five thousand four hundred and five pounds.[106] The expense of trade and transportation would greatly reduce the net profits. Ogden's expedition of 1828-1829 returned a profit of three thousand pounds, and the Snake River brigade of 1826 cleared one hundred per cent.[107]

McLoughlin stated that the Northwest Company in 1814 cleared seventy-five thousand pounds, and that this was its most profitable year.[108] Lord Selkirk, who was hostile to this company, stated that its annual gross returns amounted to one hundred fifty thousand pounds. He estimated the cost of the goods sent into the fur country as ten thousand pounds and wages at ninety thousand pounds. Wages, however, were paid in goods at a great advance over the first cost and as the

---

eight years only four per cent. Since then half yearly dividends of five per cent with bonus of ten per cent from 1828 to 1832 and since that bonus of six per cent until last year none was paid."

[104] Great Britain, House of Commons, *Report of Committee on Hudson's Bay Company*, 1857. 326.

[105] Letter of February 1, 1830. McLeod, *Journals*.

[106] Mayne (R. C.) *Four Years in British Columbia and Vancouver Island*, London, 1826, 185.

[107] McLoughlin to Governor Simpson. Fort Vancouver, August 8, 1826 in McLeod, *Journals*.

[108] Letter of February 1, 1830, in McLeod, *Journals*.

employees transported the goods into the interior without additional pay the advance was all profit. An extreme example was rum that cost twenty-five cents a quart and sold for eight dollars in the interior.[109] This estimate of profit would not be far different from McLoughlin's.

Among the American traders profits and losses were often greater than with the British companies. This was due to the lack of capital, to inferior organization, and to a greater willingness to take a chance. In 1822 a keel boat belonging to the Rocky Mountain Fur Company sank with all its merchandise worth ten thousand dollars which was half the company's resources.[110] During the five years following, however, General Ashley sold in St. Louis five hundred packs of beaver worth more than a quarter of a million dollars.[111] His profits were large for he paid for furs with sugar at a dollar a pound, gunpowder at a dollar and thirty cents, rum diluted with a large quantity of water at thirteen dollars and fifty cents per gallon, and other goods at proportionate prices.[112] So large were the profits that within five years Ashley rose from poverty to wealth.

Most of the books of Astor's American Fur Company have been destroyed,[113] but we know his fortune was acquired in the fur trade. Ramsey Crooks who succeed-

109 Selkirk, *A Sketch of the British Fur Trade in North America: with Observations relative to the Northwest Company of Montreal*, London, 1816, 36-41, cited by Davidson, 235.

110 Chittenden, *opus citra*, i, 263.

111 *Ibid.*, 281.

112 *Ibid.*, chapter i. See also letter of W. H. Ashley to Bernard Pratte and Company. October 14, 1826, in Pierre Chouteau, *Collections* which gives complete list of prices.

113 Only a few volumes of Astor's *Journals* and *Ledgers* have escaped destruction. They are in the Canadian Archives.

ed him became wealthy but lost much of his fortune in the hard years following 1837. The early fortunes of St. Louis were all made in the fur trade. Bernard Pratte, Robert Campbell, Elizabeth Ashley, Bernard Berthold, Louis Clamorgan, Pierre and Auguste Chouteau, and a number of other Chouteaus, the Sarpys, the Valles, the Papiers, and W. G. and G. W. Ewing, were the richest citizens of St. Louis in the middle of the nineteenth century,[114] and their names make a roll call of prominent fur traders.

Those who failed in the fur trade have largely been forgotten. Only a few who afterwards retrieved their failures or distinguished themselves in other ways have left a name. Jim Bridger and Jedediah Smith are remembered as great explorers, and there are many others of their kind whose names shine with only less luster.

The successful fur trader was characterized by hardiness and daring combined with a relentless disregard of Indians and competitors.[115] He obstructed with all his powers the settlement of the Northwest in order to preserve his business. In spite of his unconventional moral standards and his hard cruelty there is a romantic interest in him and his exploits that grows as the last of his kind are passing away.

P. C. P.

[114] St. Louis *Intelligencer*, September 20, 1851.

[115] The Reverend Beaver, an Episcopalian missionary to the Northwest, wrote: "God knows that I speak the conviction of my mind: and may he forgive me if I speak unadvisedly, when I state my belief, that the life of an Indian was never yet by a trapper put in competition with a beaver skin." McLeod, *Journals*, 136. Mr. Beaver did not get along well with McLoughlin, but his testimony is in accord with the spirit of the fur hunters.

Life of John Work

John Work, whose journal is here for the first time published, was a clerk and chief trader of the Hudson's Bay Company; a native of the north of Ireland and of Scotch-Irish descent. The original name was Wark, but the subject of this sketch changed it to Work. He entered the employ of the Hudson's Bay Company in 1814, serving east of the mountains for eight years; principally at York Factory and other posts in the northern part of Hudson's Bay. His name appears as numbers 421, 327, and 264 respectively, on the lists of employees of the Hudson's Bay Company in North America for the years 1821-2, 1822-3, and 1823-4.

He left York Factory on Hudson's Bay on July 18, 1823, with the brigade under charge of Chief Trader, Peter Skene Ogden, for Fort George.[116] From 1823 to 1832 he was variously stationed at Fort George (Astoria) Spokane House, Fort Colville, Fort Vancouver, and other posts. During these years much of his time was spent on trading and trapping expeditions where he underwent privations and perils similar to those related in the *Journal* here published.

Work's journal of the trip from York Factory to Fort George (July 18, 1823, to November 17, 1824) shows his powers of observation. He describes with

[116] *Journals* of John Work (9). *Trading expedition under C. F. Ogden from near Oxford House to Columbia and Fort George,* July 18, 1823 – November 17, 1824. Copy in Canadian Archives, Ottawa. These journals are contained in thirteen folios in cartons labeled H. B. C. – P. C. P.

Ogden did not become a chief factor until 1834. – W. S. L.

intelligence the whole country through which he traveled. His journey led him by Spokane House from which post he and Finan McDonald started on August 30, 1824, with a party of thirteen men to trade with the Flathead Indians. This was Work's first venture into the Flathead country. He found the natives friendly and carried on a profitable trade with them. Upon his return to Spokane he continued his journey and arrived at Fort George in the fall. On November 18, 1824, the day after his arrival at Fort George, Work started "to the northward . . . to discover entrance to Fraser's River."

The next year, on June 21, 1825, he started out as a member of the Interior Brigade under the command of John McLeod,[117] from Fort Vancouver, to trade with the Flatheads and other tribes in the valley of Clark's Fork. The trade seems to have been brisk although Work complained that it was not as large as the year before. On December 22, Work reported that there were sent to Spokane eleven hundred thirty-eight beaver, thirteen hundred eighty-five rats besides a number of elk, deer, marten, mink, and other furs. On March 19, 1826, he reported the departure of sixty-two horses loaded with furs and sundries, and on April 18, he, with Francis Ermatinger and Finan McDonald, started with a boat load of furs for Okanagan.

In July, 1826, Work started with another expedition under the command of William Connelly, who had the year before been made chief factor,[118] to trade in the

[117] *Trading Expedition made by the Interior Brigade from Fort Vancouver under command of McLeod,* June 21, 1825-June 12, 1826.—P. C. P.

[118] *Statement of commissioned officers H. B. C. . .* Copy in Canadian Archives. M. 865.—P. C. P.

valley of Clark's Fork.[119] Douglas, the botanist, accompanied the expedition in search of plants and seeds.[120] On July 17, a party composed of Archibald Macdonald, James Douglas, F. Annance, David Douglas, and Work accompanied by an interpreter and twenty-eight men started to the Nez Percés to trade for horses. On their return from this expedition the party set out for the trade with the Flatheads. Soon after this, Work wrote that the Flatheads "had seen a party of Americans during the summer" and that these Americans were "loaded with trading goods, and that they were going to build in the fall on the upper waters of the Missouri." This report of American competition seems to have been exaggerated, for a few days later Work learned from some Nez Percés "that the Indians are at the Horse Plains [Plains, Montana] and that a lodge of Americans are with them." He was also informed that the Americans had only tobacco to trade. The Nez Percés, he learned, were camped a little farther to the east at Camas. At this time Work met some of the Flathead chiefs who were soon to be seekers of the Christian religion, notably Gros Pied, and Grand Visage.

The Americans used every effort to win over the Flatheads. They invited the chiefs to visit their great chief, Ashley, who they said was just across the mountains with a vast quantity of supplies. They also reported that their countrymen were sending five ship loads of goods to the Columbia.[121]

[119] *Trading expedition for interior under command of Connelly*, July 5, 1826, 12. Copy in Canadian Archives. – P. C. P.

[120] David Douglas, *Journal* . . . 1823-1827, London, 1914, 64. – P. C. P.

[121] Evidently Rocky Mountain Fur Company traders. – P. C. P.

It is not certain how many furs the Americans got, but the Hudson's Bay party obtained only two hundred sixty-seven beaver and a few muskrats from the Flatheads. From the Kootenais, however, who had not traded with the Americans, they traded three hundred ninety-two beaver and five hundred rats besides other furs.

After this Flathead expedition of 1826, Work's *Journals* deal mostly with activities along the Columbia[122] until the spring of 1831 when he became a chief trader and succeeded Ogden in charge of the Snake River brigade.[123] On April 21 of that year he started up the Snake River and across country to the valley of the Great Salt Lake. Two years before Peter Skene Ogden had hunted this region with good success. Work had high hopes of many beaver but was disappointed. The Blackfoot Indians bothered him a great deal and after many misfortunes Work turned north to John Day's River in Idaho and then back to the Nez Percés. On this expedition he traveled more than a thousand miles.[124]

From this expedition Work returned to Fort Nez Percé [Walla Walla] on July 19, 1831, and one month later on August 18, he started on the great trading and trapping expedition to the Flathead and Blackfoot Indians which is published in this volume.

Work returned to Fort Vancouver on July 27, 1832, and less than a month after this strenuous trip, on Au-

122 Work's *Journals* describe an *Expedition from Fort Colville to Okanagan*, May 20 - Aug. 18, 1828, 14. – P. C. P.

123 Washington Historical Society *Quarterly*, i, 263. – W. S. L.

124 *Hunting and Trading Expedition down Snake River. . . to Utah and Return to Nez Percés*, April 21-July 19, 1831. Oregon Historical Society *Quarterly*, xiii, 363-371; xiv, 280-314.

gust 17, he set out on an expedition to "Bonaventura Valley" via Ogden's River, accompanied by J. T. Larocque.[125] This expedition promised well but Work soon found that a Hudson's Bay Company's brigade that had been sent along the coast had turned towards the interior and obtained several hundred beaver, that should have gone to his party. He also found that a party of Americans under a man named Young had carried on a large trade with the Indians. When he reached California Work found the Indians hostile, influenced as he supposed by the Spaniards. His party was overcome by sickness and was unsuccessful in the search for beaver. The Russians would sell no supplies and hindered the party in every way possible. Work, discouraged, returned to Vancouver April 2, 1833. The next day he set out on an expedition down the Snake River which occupied the whole summer.[126] This expedition suffered much from fever and thieving Indians. Very few pelts were obtained.

The next year Work led a party for a six weeks hunt to the Umpqua country, south of Vancouver. His trading on this trip was also not very successful.[127]

From 1834-1835, Work was in charge of the Hudson's Bay Company's coast shipping, with headquarters at Vancouver. On December 11, 1834, he left Vancouver by steamer to trade along the Northwest coast.[128] The Russians prevented him from establishing a post,

[125] *Hunting Expedition to Bonaventura Valley by Way of Ogden's River*, August 17, 1832-April 2, 1833.—P. C. P.

[126] *Hunting Expedition down Snake River*, April 3-October 31, 1833.—P. C. P.

[127] *Trading and Hunting trip to the southward from Fort Vancouver*, May 22-July 10, 1834.—P. C. P.

[128] *Expedition to Northwest Coast*, December 11, 1834-June 25, 1835.—P. C. P.

and he found the Indians demanding an exorbitant price for their furs. He believed they were holding back, waiting for American traders. Work paid a high price rather than run the risk of allowing competitors to get the pelts and he thereby hoped to discourage any further competition. These Indians would even refuse seven blankets with rum, molasses, and rice for one sea otter. In March, 1835, Captain Allen of the American ship Europa arrived with a fine assortment of goods and the bidding became quite serious and prices went up enormously. Work complained of the American methods of trade which he was compelled to imitate. In spite of his difficulties Work had obtained about three thousand beaver, two thousand martens, eight hundred mink, two hundred sea otter and many other varieties of fur.

From 1835 to 1849 Work was in charge of the Hudson's Bay Company's business at Fort Simpson. It was not, however, until 1846 that he was promoted to the office of chief factor. He had long felt that he was treated unfairly,[129] and regarded this as only a tardy recognition of his services.

While in the Columbia River district John Work was assigned to superintend the erection of new Fort Colville on the site selected by Governor Simpson, and planted there one of the first farms west of the mountains. In 1849, with James Douglas and a Mr. Ross, he surveyed and mapped some four thousand acres at the Cowlitz Prairie settlement, in what is now the state of Washington.

In 1850 he formed, with Peter Skene Ogden and James (afterwards Sir James) Douglas, the Board of

129 See letter to Edward Ermatinger, Appendix. – P. C. P.

Managers of the Columbia department of the Hudson's Bay Company. He was a member of the first government and legislative council of Vancouver Island from 1857 up to the time of his death, and became one of the first farmers in the Victoria district. The John Work mentioned as being at Fort Vancouver in 1860, when the Hudson's Bay Company withdrew from that post was a nephew. John Work died in the employ of the Hudson's Bay Company at Victoria, British Columbia, December 23, 1861, at the age of seventy. He was buried from the old fort yard near the present post office building at Victoria.

John Work has been described as a man of very strong physique, of great endurance, and of a very practical mind. His strict integrity, which inspired confidence and commanded respect, was associated with a most kindly disposition which won all hearts. He was very well thought of among all the Hudson's Bay Company officials in the Columbia River district,[130] and held the respect and gratitude of David Douglas, the great botanist whom he often assisted in collecting plants and seeds.[131] A contemporary characterized him as a "tender hearted, generous Irishman who often amused his associates by his murder of the French

[130] "Our friend Work succeeds me in the Snake country, I accompanied him as far as Nez Percés and gave him a fair starting – surely this man deserves a more substantial reward than he now enjoys; it is an unpleasant situation he fills, I wish him every success but it is all a lottery." Letter, Peter Skene Ogden to John McLeod, March 10, 1831. Washington Historical Society *Quarterly*, i, 263. – W. S. L.

[131] David Douglas, *Journal*, speaks of the "many good offices" he had from Work, 65. He mentions that Work "sent me a few seeds from the interior last November, and furnished me with some valuable information about the plants and mountain sheep in this neighborhood [mouth of Spokane River]" 161: "my old friend Mr. John Work," 180. – P. C. P.

tongue." Mr. A. C. Anderson in a brief biography emphasized his kindly disposition. The Victoria *Colonist* said of him: "Nothing pleased him more than to be surrounded by children, by whom he was especially beloved. His end was a fitting close of a life of integrity and benevolence."[132]

John Work's wife was Susette Legace, a Spokane half-breed girl, a niece of old Charles Legace, by whom he had five daughters and one son. One of these daughters married Dr. William Fraser Tolmie of Fort Nisqually; another married the late Edward Huggins of Nisqually and Tacoma, Washington; another married Chief Trader Roderick Finlayson; and a fourth married Mr. James A. Grahame, afterwards Chief Commissioner of the Hudson's Bay Company.

The district visited by Work on the expedition of 1831-1832, that of the Blackfoot and Snake River Indians, was extremely dangerous.[133] Hunting and trapping was carried on under continued surveillance from hostile Indians who were constantly stealing traps, horses, and attacking isolated trappers, and even making assaults on the main party. Horses had to be carefully herded, and a guard constantly maintained to prevent their capture by Indian raiders. Under these conditions the party of necessity had to assume something of the character of a military body in enemy country.

Although the number of men in the expedition leaving Fort Vancouver is omitted in the *Journal*, from details elsewhere given, it is apparent that the party

132 Bancroft, *The Northwest Coast*, ii, 464. – W. S. L.

133 "I escaped with my scalp last year. I doubt much whether I shall be so fortunate this trip." Letter of John Work, September 6, 1831. Appendix. The Crows and Blackfeet were particularly hostile to all whites at this time, both British and American. – W. S. L.

consisted of thirty-five or forty men; eight or ten to a boat. Most of these men were veterans in the Company's employ and many of them had already served on one or more previous expeditions to the Snake River country. Indians and perhaps a few white trappers were probably added to the party at Fort Nez Percé. So far as the editors can ascertain, the names of the party, augmented at Fort Nez Percé, were as follows:

Barssonette, L.
Birnie, P.
Blonte, A., trapper, probably A. Plante; deserted October 24, 1831.
Boisvert, Louis (also S. Boisverte, also Boisant, Bairvent, Baisvent), trapper.[134]
Bte (Baptiste), J. J., trapper.[135]
Burdod, trapper; also Budard. He and his family with him.
Carney; also Curry, possibly same as Champagne.
Champagne; also Chamfrouge, Chamfronge, possibly Carney.
Cloutier; also J. Claudin, Clantin, I. Clouture; J. Clantin in Bancroft MS. Trapper killed by Blackfeet October 31, 1831.
Cook, R.
Coving, J., trapper.
Desland, J., wounded November 24.
Dubruille, Bt., a member of Work's 1830-1831 expedition.
Dumais, A., the same as A. Dumerais of the 1830-1831 expedition. Trapper drowned in Snake River, July 19, 1832.
Faul, J., also spelled Paul.
Favel, A., trapper.
Finlay, Abraham, trapper.
Finlay, M., trapper; deserted October 24, 1831.
Finlay, O., deserted October 24, 1831.[136]

[134] An old Hudson's Bay Company employee whose name appears as number 336 on the lists for 1823-4. Probably identical with Louis Boivers, a settler of French Prairie, Oregon, who opposed the Provisional Government organization at Champoeg, May 2, 1843. – W. S. L.

[135] Possibly J. Bt'e Belleau, a voyageur, who arrived on the Tonquin in 1811; see Franchere's *Narrative*, 31; his name appears as numbers 1562 and 450 in the lists of 1821-3 and 1822-3. – W. S. L.

Gadipre, Bt., a trapper.

Gaudefoux Bt. (also as Gadif).

Grosbin, C.

Grell, P.

Houle, A., a trapper who started with Work but became ill and was left behind at Fort Walla Walla, September 9, 1831.

Kanota, L. variously spelled Kanata, Kanola, Kanotti, etc., in copies of Work's *Journals*; an old Hudson's Bay Company employee, frequently accompanying Mr. Work on his trapping expeditions.[137]

La Busche, variously spelled Le Buche, La Bruh, La Brash, La Buche, La Bunte, Le Brute, Le Burte, etc. A guide.[138]

Lefort, M. (M. Lefat).

[136] A. Finlay, O. Finlay, and M. Finlay were sons or descendants of old Jacco Raphael Finlay, an old Northwest and Hudson's Bay Company employee, operating as an independent fur trader and trapper in the Kootenai and Flathead Indian country, 1806-9, and a half-breed son of James Finlay, a Northwesterner. Jacco married east of the mountains and most of his children were born in the vicinity of Edmonton. He was possibly the founder of Spokane House in the summer of 1810, and died there on May 20, 1828. His name is preserved in Jacco, or Jocko Creek, Missoula County, Montana. David Douglas in his *Journal*, 63, 169, gives the better French spelling of Jacques, and this is found on Wilkes map of 1843. – P. C. P. Jacco Finlay and his sons were reputed to be the best woodsmen, trappers, and hunters in the Northwest. Compare his single kill of three buffalo with the hunting results of the entire party in the days immediately preceding and following. M. Plante, O. Finlay, and M. Finlay were with John Work in 1830, Oregon Historical Society *Quarterly*, xiii, 369, and in 1831; *ibid.*, xiv, 284-299. – W. S. L.

Francois Finlay or Benetsee, who discovered gold in Montana, was a three-quarter breed of this family. Gold Creek was first named "Benetsee Creek" after him, and was given its present name by the members of the government railroad survey under Governor Stevens. Bancroft's *History of Washington, Idaho, and Montana*, 611. – W. S. L. See also *Mississippi Valley Historical Review*, iv, 87 ff. – P. C. P.

[137] Oregon Historical Society *Quarterly*, xiii, 366. – W. S. L. Kanota was a Hawaiian. The early fur traders to the Northwest coast often went by sea around Cape Horn to the Sandwich Islands. There they frequently enlisted natives for the expedition to the Oregon country. – P. C. P.

[138] This old chief is mentioned in Mr. Work's earlier *Journal* of December, 1825; see Washington Historical Society *Quarterly*, v, 110, 186-9; vi, 40. He is not to be confounded with La Bonte, the Astorian of Irving's *Astoria*, xxxvii, who was a member of Work's earlier expeditions. – W. S. L.

Letandre, E., also spelled Letude, Latude, Litude, Letaude, Leteude, Lateudre, etc. Trapper killed by Blackfeet, October 31, 1831.

Longtin, A., trapper.

Lorange, J. S., also J. Laurin and J. Lausin, trapper.

Masson, A., Mapir in Bancroft MS.

Norty, boy sick and left behind September 8.

Old Indian Charley, who accompanied Mr. Work on previous expeditions to the Flathead country, 1825-6.[139]

Osie.

Paus, G.; also G. Paris.

Payette, Francis.[140]

Pearce.

Pinet; also Pichette.

Plante, C., trapper, half-breed, deserted October 24, 1831.

Plante, M., half-breed trapper. Name is variously spelled Plant and Planti.[141]

Plante's, M., brother-in-law, a youth of 16 years. Poisoned by hemlock, March 21, 1832.

Quintal, Laurent; also spelled Quintall in Bancroft MS.[142]

Rayburn, J. possibly same as J. Reyhn, a trapper.

---

139 Washington Historical Society *Quarterly*, v, 98, 104-5, 171; vi, 31, 33-5. – W. S. L.

140 Payette was a responsible employee, whose name appears as numbers 1230, 1021, and 738 in the Hudson's Bay Company's lists for the years 1821-4. He was originally a Northwesterner, and in the Snake River with Mr. McKenzie in 1818. He ranked as an interpreter and was stationed with the Kootenais in 1830, and was later promoted to postmaster at £75 per annum and stationed at Forts Hall and Boise in 1839-41; and as postmaster and clerk in the Snake River expedition, Forts Hall and Borssie, 1842 and 1843. His name is preserved in the state of Idaho in the town of Payette, Payette River, and Payette Lake. – W. S. L.

141 Plante was a trapper with John Work on the Snake River expedition of 1830. Oregon Historical Society *Quarterly*, xiii, 369, and in the expedition of 1830-1; deserted October 24, 1831, rejoined the party January 20, 1832. *Ibid.*, xiv, 290. He was drowned in the Snake River, July 19, 1832. – W. S. L.

142 Numbered 1274 in Hudson's Bay Company's list for 1821-2, 1060 for 1822-3, and 870 for 1823-4. He was with Alexander Ross on the Snake River expedition of 1824, who refers to him as "the sly dog Laurent . . . a more headstrong, discordant, ill-designing set of rascals than form this

Raymond, Wm., trapper, no. 329 in the Hudson's Bay Company's list of 1821-22 and 254 in list of 1822-23; mortally wounded January 10, 1832, died March 14, 1832.

Rodin, a trapper.

Rondeau, C., Charles Rondeau, numbers 1305 and 1090 on the lists of employees of the Hudson's Bay Company for 1821-2 and 1822-3. He settled at French Prairie and voted against the Americans, May 2, 1843.

Rondeau, L., trapper, number 1293 on the Hudson's Bay Company's list for 1821-2 and 1070 for 1822-3; taken sick and left at Fort Walla Walla September 9, 1831, rejoined the party January 20, 1832.

Ross, Gilbert.

Satakays, P.

Silbert; possibly same as Gilbert Ross above.

Smith, T., trapper.

Soteaux, trapper; lost July 8, 1832, still missing July 16. Probably died in the mountains.[143]

Toupe, J.

A Flathead Indian, mortally wounded November 24, 1831.

Walla Walla Indian, mortally wounded by Blackfeet, January 30, 1832, died February 2.

John Work's "little Walla Walla housekeeper;" wounded by the Blackfeet, January 30, 1832.

In addition to those whose names are given or who are otherwise described there were a number of Indian and half-breed women and children, squaws and children of the Indian hunters and the white traders and trappers. Work was accompanied by his three small daughters who were probably cared for by his Walla Walla housekeeper.

The Snake River brigades were devoted primarily

camp God never permitted together in the fur trade." Oregon Historical Society *Quarterly*, xiv, 376. – W. S. L.

[143] Work says in his *Journal of a Hunting Expedition to Bonaventura Valley by Way of Ogden's River*, August 17, 1832-April 2, 1833: – on August 22, 1832, "Hear that Soteaux whom we lost July 8 murdered by the Snakes."

to the search for beaver. Each expedition had among its personnel some traders, clerks, and store keepers who looked after the trading goods such as guns, powder, balls, blankets, knives, axes, mirrors, and other articles which the Indian prized and for which he was willing to exchange the results of his hunting and trapping.

The hunters and trappers were more numerous than the traders, and a party of trappers was usually composed of Indians, French Canadians, and mixed breeds. When a good beaver stream was found the party camped until the supply of beaver was exhausted. Work's expedition of 1831-1832, however, found few good beaver streams and was almost constantly on the move. In most cases when the camp was not moved each day the failure to move was due to bad weather or danger from the Indians.

It is typical of the conditions of the fur trade that while Mr. Work, at the close of his *Journal*, makes a careful statement and accounting of the horses lost during the expedition, no mention whatever is made of the casualties among his men. During the course of his narrative, however, he noted the killing of eight different men. Annual drafts of fresh men were necessary to keep up these constant losses from sickness, accident, and violent death among the employees in the Indian country.

John Work spelled better than many of his contemporaries. There is, however, a considerable variation in his spelling of names, particularly in his spelling of French or Indian names. Most of his party probably

---

On September 21 he wrote, "Any Indian found with Soteaux's property to be punished instantly." – P. C. P.

did not know how to spell and Work was not intimately enough acquainted with the French and Indian tongues to spell the names accurately from merely hearing them pronounced. John Work's *Journals* were written nearly a hundred years ago and in places the ink is faded until the words can hardly be deciphered. This may also account for some of the variations in spelling.

Work's daughter, Mrs. W. F. Tolmie, and her children of Victoria, British Columbia, seem to have fallen heir to many of his papers. A number of his journals are now in the Provincial Library at Victoria, British Columbia, and they have been frequently cited by Hubert Howe Bancroft, the historian. Relative to their historical value Mr. Bancroft writes: "To none of the Hudson's Bay Company officers is posterity more indebted than to John Work whose journals of various expeditions, nowhere else recorded, fill a gap in history."

Portions of John Work's *Journals* 1825 and 1826, edited by Mr. T. C. Elliott, have heretofore appeared in the Washington Historical Society *Quarterly*, iii, 198-228; v, 83-115, 258-287; vi, 26-49. Another journal covering a trip from Fort Colville to Vancouver and return (1828) recently appeared in the Washington Historical Society *Quarterly*, xi, 104-114. Extracts from Work's *Journals of the Oregon and Snake River Expedition of 1830-1831*, also edited by Mr. T. C. Elliott, have appeared in the Oregon Historical Society *Quarterly*, xiii, 363-371; xiv, 280-314. A summary of this *Journal* appears in Bancroft's *History of the Northwest Coast*, ii, 516-519. The journal of his trip southward (1834) mentioned in Bancroft's *History of the*

Northwest Coast, ii, 526-9, will shortly appear in the Oregon Historical Society *Quarterly* with the editorial notes of Mr. Lesie M. Scott.

The original of the *Journal* of the expedition of 1831-1832 is now in the Provincial Library at Victoria, British Columbia. An abstract of it was made for Hubert Howe Bancroft. Mr. R. E. Gosnell of the Provincial Library at Victoria made a copy for the Canadian Archives in 1908. At about the same time he prepared a copy for Professor E. S. Meany of the University of Washington. This copy is used for the text printed in this volume. The well known accuracy of Mr. Gosnell's work makes it unnecessary for the editors to make any further explanation regarding the faithfulness of the copy herein printed.

The editors have taken the liberty of making some changes in the spelling of the original manuscript, such as Satd.y, Sund.y and Mond.y. Work followed no uniform method of spelling, so the editors thought it best to give the full spelling of the days of the week.

The Journal of John Work

THURSDAY, AUGUST 18, 1831. Left Vancouver[144] and joined the Snake Expedition[145] men at the [lower] sawmill, where they were sent a few days ago to drink the regale.[146] Some of the men being in liquor I deferred starting till tomorrow. The party consists of [ ][147] men in four boats. Four of the men, M. Plante, L. Quintal, A. Masson, and I. Clouture,[148] are sick with the fever.[149] They are very ill, but it is expected they will get better on experiencing a change of climate above the cascades [The Doctor furnished me

---

144 Vancouver. Fort Vancouver on the Columbia River, the headquarters of the Hudson's Bay Company in the Northwest. – W. S. L.

145 Snake Expedition. It was the custom of the Hudson's Bay Company to send expeditions into the Snake River country to trade with the Indians and to trap. The expedition of 1831 planned a more extensive trip than usual across the present state of Idaho and into western Montana. Professor C. J. Brosnan, of the University of Idaho, has made a study of the Snake River brigades and the results of his labors will probably soon be published. – P. C. P.

146 Regales. By long established custom, the men, mostly French-Canadian half-breeds, were supplied with liquor and given a few days vacation prior to their departure on one of these expeditions. To avoid any disturbance of the people at the Fort the men were required to camp for these regales at some distance from the Fort. The lower mill was about four miles from the trading post. This second saw mill must have been erected some time prior to this date. – W. S. L.

147 Four boats would ordinarily hold not more than forty men. In the course of his narrative Work refers to sixty different people. These include, besides the French and Scotch trappers and traders, a number of Indians, men, women, and children.

148 For information regarding the men of Work's party see pages 61-65.

149 Malaria fever and ague such as afflicted the first settlers in the Mississippi River valley, doubtlessly spread by the mosquitoes in the spring. The

with a small quantity of medicine for them].[150] In the evening two more of the men, A. Houle and W. Raymure, were taken ill, but I suppose it to be the effect of liquor.

FRIDAY, AUGUST 19. Proceeded up the river to above the steep rocks,[151] when we put ashore in the evening for the night. The sick men, if anything, worse. It is the fever the two taken ill yesterday have.

SATURDAY, July [August] 20. Embarked at an early hour but soon had to put ashore on account of a strong head wind, which did not abate till the afternoon, and then some of the sick were so ill that we could not proceed. Two more of the men, Bt. Gaudifoux and Louis Kanota, taken ill. Some of the others are very ill and one or two of them are getting better.

SUNDAY, August 21. Continued our route up the river to the cascades, and carried the cargoes part of the way across the portage.[152] Some of the sick men very ill and some of them a little better.

MONDAY, August 22. Carried the cargoes across the portage by midday, and proceeded up the river with a sail wind. The sick men continued the same.

---

ague first appeared on the Pacific Coast in 1830. Lee and Frost, *Ten Years in Oregon*, New York, 1844, 108.

"An intermittent fever was raging at Vancouver when I left, this scourge was carrying off the few wretched natives who escaped last year, it had also attacked several of the people about the establishment. My people did not escape it, several of them were taken ill, and some of them remained so badly that I am obliged to leave them here as they are not able to proceed, this I much regret as my numbers at first were too weak." *Letter*, John Work, Sept. 6, 1831. *Ibid.*, 263. – W. S. L.

150 Bancroft MS. The doctor must have turned back at the mill for he receives no further mention in the *Journal*. – P. C. P.

151 Locally called "Cape Horn." – T. C. ELLIOTT.

152 This portage was on the north side of the Columbia River where the first portage railroad was built about thirty years later. – T. C. E.

TUESDAY, August 23. The weather too stormy to admit of our marching, so that we did not stir all day. Some of the sick men very ill, Quintal, M. Plante, Raymure, and A. Houle are becoming very weak. I much regret that they came away from Vancouver, it is impossible to attend them as they ought to be on the voyage, and what little medicine I had will soon be done. I am sorry I did not send them back from the cascades, but I was still in hopes they would get better, moreover, I could not send them back without some healthy men with them (as I could not risk them alone) and that would weaken my party too much.

WEDNESDAY, August 24. Continued up the river with a strong sail wind to the Dalles, and with the assistance of Indians carried the goods to the sand half way across the portage.[153] The sick people continue the same, the worst ones weakening again.[154]

THURSDAY, August 25. Had the goods carried across the portage early in the morning, but it was past midday before the boats were got up to the head of the party [portage].[155] We then proceeded to the little Dalles, where we had also to make a portage,[156] and with the assistance of Indians had the baggage all across in the evening. Another of the men, L. Rondeau, was taken ill with the fever yesterday, and today is very bad. The others still continue ill, and are becoming very

153 This portage was on the south side of the Columbia where the Dalles-Celilo Canal has since been built. It was around Five Mile Rapids, or the Lower Dalles. – T. C. E.

154 "The worst ones weakening again." Bancroft MS. reads. "The wind was weakening again." This makes better sense. – P. C. P.

155 Bancroft MS. reads "portage" in place of "party." – P. C. P.

156 This portage was also on the south side of the river and around the upper Dalles or Nine Mile Rapids. – T. C. E.

weak, except Gadifoux and Kanota, who are getting better.

FRIDAY, August 26. Proceeded to the Chutes,[157] and had the baggage and boats (with the help of Indians) across the portage by noon. Some time was lost gumming the boats, when we proceeded up the river with a strong sail wind, it blew so fresh that we had to put ashore for an hour. We reached opposite Mr. Day's River[158] where we encamped in the evening. Another of the men, Osie, taken sick with the fever. So many of the men falling ill is a serious affair. The only thing we can do is to push on as expeditiously as possible.

SATURDAY, August 27. Continued on up the river with a sail wind to below Big Island,[159] where we encamped. Another man, Bt. Dubruille took ill with the fever. A. Houle had got a little better and had begun to work a little against my advice, and is again fallen back worse than he was at first.

SUNDAY, August 28. We had a sail wind which carried us to near Utalle[160] River, where we encamped late in the evening. The sick men continuing the same.

MONDAY, August 29. Warm, calm weather.

Continued our route and encamped a little below the

157 The "Chutes" were the Celilo Falls. The portage here was usually on the north side of the river. – T. C. E.

158 In Bancroft MS. "Jeays" – The John Day's River of Oregon – so named for John Day – the Kentucky trapper with the Astor party who died in 1819 from the hardships he encountered in the mountains of Idaho. A small creek in Idaho and one in Wyoming also bear his name. Oregon Historical Society *Quarterly*, xiv, 380; xvii, 375. He was highly esteemed by his associates. – W. S. L.

159 Big Island, often called Long Island by the fur traders and early settlers, is now called Blalock's Island for the late Dr. Blalock of pioneer railroad fame, one of the early settlers of Walla Walla, Washington. – T. C. E.

160 Utalle – Umatilla rapids, below mouth of river of that name. – T. C. E.

fort.[161] Having no wind this was a hard day's work on the people. The heat was hard on the sick people, some of them who had got a little better relapsed again. It was lucky the weather was grown really cool, had it been warm it would likely have caused the death of some of our sick men.

TUESDAY, August 30. Had a little breeze of wind [in the morning][162] and reached the fort to breakfast, and found Mr. McGillivray[163] and people all well. Some men who were sent from Vancouver to Colville[164] with letters and for some supplies of horses and horse agents passed here on the [ ] inst., and have not yet returned, it is probable they are detained till the Colville people return from the F[lat]head summer trade.[165]

---

[161] Fort Nez Percé [or Walla Walla] at the mouth of the Walla Walla River which had been established in 1818 by Donald MacKenzie and Alexander Ross. – W. S. L.

[162] Bancroft MS.

[163] Simon McGillivray, clerk in charge of the fort, was a son of William, an old Northwesterner. Simon McGillivray served with the Canadian chasseurs in the War of 1812 and was present at the capture of Mackinac. In 1813 he entered the employ of the Northwest Company, arriving in the Columbia River district with the fall brigade and wintering at Fort Okanogan, 1813-4. See Cox's Columbia River, i, 238, 130-131. On the union of the two companies in 1821 he became a chief trader of the Hudson's Bay Company. His name appears as nos. 42, 28, and 27 respectively on the lists of employees of the company for the years 1821-2, 1822-3, and 1823-4. In a letter by J. E. Harriott, dated Fort Vancouver, February 25, 1831, appearing in Washington Historical Society *Quarterly*, i, 260, 261, we find: "Mr. Simon McGillivray reached this on the 6th Jan[uar]y and after regaling himself a few days at this place took his departure for Walla Walla to replace Mr. Barnston." By minutes of council for 1831 he was assigned to the New Caledonia department for 1832. – W. S. L.

[164] Fort Colville on the upper Columbia some distance below the mouth of Clark's Fork. This fort was a sort of clearing house for the trade with the Indians to the east. See Appendix for Work's account of his prospects. – P. C. P.

[165] The Flathead summer trade was an important asset to the Northwest Company and was continued by the Hudson's Bay Company after it ab-

WEDNESDAY, August 31. Stormy weather.

We require one hundred and twenty horses to equip our party, and there are only about eighty here, so that we still want about forty horses. Whether that number will be obtained from Colville[166] I cannot say. Some of the sick men very ill, M. Plante was nearly dying. Some of them who had got a little better have relapsed again.

THURSDAY, September 1. Very little doing. The sick continue the same, some of them becoming very weak.

FRIDAY, September 2. Some of the sick men a little better, others of them very ill. Late in the evening the men arrived from Colville with all the supplies required except horses, of which they have brought only twenty-four, and these so lean that they will be of little or no service to us this year. One was left sick by the way.

SATURDAY, September 3. Employed giving out the people supplies and provisions and other things. Our sick men getting a very little better.

SUNDAY, September 4. Employed as yesterday. The sick men continuing much the same.

MONDAY, September 5. A number of the horses

sorbed the Northwest Company in 1821. David Thompson apparently realized the potential importance of this trade when he stopped in the Kootenai country in 1809. On the east side of Lake Pend d'Oreille he built "Kullyspel" House and on Clark's Fork above the site of Thompson Falls, Montana, he built Saleesh House. Coues, *Journals of Alexander Henry and of David Thompson*, ii, 606 n.

The term Flathead probably refers to the various tribes of the Salishan family that inhabited the basin of Clark's Fork of the Columbia River. – P. C. P.

166 Fort Colville was near enough the Nez Percés to carry on a trade in horses with that tribe of horsemen. – P. C. P.

strayed and could not be found which deterred me from giving them to the people as intended.

TUESDAY, September 6. It was so late in the day before the horses were found that I could not deliver them today either.

WEDNESDAY, September 7. It was near noon when some of the horses who had strayed again were collected, after which we were busily employed delivering them to the people, and a difficult job it is as there are not enough of horses, and a number of what are, are of such an inferior quality that little or no work can be expected to be done with them, those received from Colville, in particular, are not only very lean but the great number of them young, unbroken horses.

THURSDAY, September 8. Gave out the remainder of the horses to the people, and part of them moved off, the others remain till tomorrow. Some of the men are badly equipped with horses, they number [ ] and that is all. There being no Indians about the place worth meeting none can be got to trade at present. Some of our sick men whom I thought would have to remain here have determined to accompany us, viz: J. B. Dubruille, A. Masson, S. Quintall, and M. Plante, they will not be persuaded to remain, and I much fear they are inadequate (though a little better) for the journey, and will most likely die on the way. I have represented the imprudence of risking themselves and the consequence likely to result from it. Two of the sick men, L. Riendeau and A. Houle, are unable to even attempt the journey, and remain, the boy Norty is also unable to go, he must remain, he was taken ill a few days ago and is in a violent fever, though he has no fits.

FRIDAY, September 9. Some of the people came back for some stray horses, and did not go away as it was late when they found them.

SATURDAY, September 10. Employed today writing letters.

SUNDAY, September 11. Left Fort Nez Percés, and at the end of five hours march, about twenty-five miles N.E. came up with the people on a fork of W. W. River.[167] Two of the horses lost, one belonging to J.

[167] Walla Walla River: Camping on Mill Creek, somewhere between the present stations of Whitman and College Place. Eighteen miles NE:-From Mill Creek, the distances or the directions given by Mr. Work for his journeys September 12-16 inclusive, must be altered to bring him out near the mouth of the Salmon River, which is considerable to the south of Fort Nez Percé. Local magnetic variances, amounting to even twenty or twenty-five degrees east, are occasionally encountered in the Columbia River district, and may explain this discrepancy; hence the editors here disregard Mr. Work's directions and are guided by his distances only. We assume that instead of taking the well-traveled Nez Percé trail towards the mouth of the Clearwater, he proceeded east across the northern edge of the Blue Mountains by another Indian trail shown on Lieutenant Symons' maps of the department of the Columbia, camping on the 12 of September on Russell's Creek. Compare herewith Peter Skene Ogden's route September, 1828, *ibid.*, xi, 381; and John Work's route August, 1839, *ibid.*, xiii, 364-5.

This route from the Walla Walla River to the Snake River was a well known Nez Percé trail, and the latter portion of Work's route was practically that taken by Joseph's band and the Nez Percés from the Imnaha and vicinity of Asotin in June, 1877, when they gathered and crossed the Snake River above the mouth of the Salmon; marched up that stream and crossing it at Craig's Ferry (Ford) camped at the rendezvous on Rocky Canyon Creek, east of the Salmon, prior to the battle of White Bird. – W. S. L.

Mr. T. C. Elliott of Walla Walla, the well known authority on the Hudson's Bay Company regime in the Columbia River district is of the firm opinion that a different and northern route was taken by the Work party and he has submitted the following:

"September 11-26. From Fort Nez Percé at the mouth of the Walla Walla River on the Columbia, Mr. Work and his party followed the regular Indian trail used by Lewis and Clark expedition when going eastward in 1806, across the hills to the Touchet River and their camp on the evening of the 12th seems to have been at the present site of Dayton, Columbia County, Wash., where Patit Creek (from petite or small creek), which

Faul and one belonging to P. Satakays. Two others were left below two days ago, which could not come on.

MONDAY, September 12. Continued our route five hours, eighteen miles N. E. to another small river, want of water was the cause of making such a long [short] [168] day's journey.

TUESDAY, September 13. Overcast but very warm weather.

Continued our journey six hours, twenty-two miles E. to another small river,[169] there was no water to encamp sooner. Many of the horses fatigued. [Two of the sick men again taken very ill; had some severe fits to-day].[170] Some of the Indians visited us in the evening and changed horses with the people.

WEDNESDAY, September 14. Cloudy, cold weather.

Proceeded on our journey two and one-half hours,

carries very little water in September, enters the Touchet River. From there the party left the Lewis and Clark party's route and followed the upper Indian trail nearer the mountains across Garfield County by what is now Columbia Center and Peola to the Snake River (Nez Percé river he calls it) a few miles below the mouth of the Clearwater (he calls it the Salmon). Crossing the river the party proceeded up on the north bank of the Clearwater, perhaps crossing to the south side further up, to where the North Fork comes in on the 24th, and then to the trail leading over the hills to Weippe prairie on the 26th. His Camas Plain is the Weippe. From there the road to the Hot Springs is the Lolo Trail with deviations; evidently they got off the trail just as the Lewis and Clark party did when coming across in the fall of 1805. This was a route not usually followed by the Hudson's Bay Company traders in going to the Snake and Missouri River country and was strange to Mr. Work."

If this is the case Work's party journeyed up the Clearwater instead of the Salmon River, crossing the north fork of the Clearwater on September 24, and proceeded up the south fork for two days when he left the river to go to Camas Plains near Weippe, Idaho. From this point Mr. J. E. Rees traces the route to Lolo Pass. – P. C. P.

168 Should be "short" as in Bancroft MS.

169 Camping on the upper Wenaha in the vicinity of Willow and Owl Creeks. – W. S. L.

170 Bancroft MS.

eight miles E. to another small river.[171] We were induced to stop earlier than usual on account of the country being burnt and dreading that we could not get grass farther on. Some more Indians visited us and traded a few horses with the people.

THURSDAY, September 15. Sultry, warm weather. Marched seven and one-half hours, twenty-five miles N. E. to N. P. River.[172] The country along the way was burnt and no grass for the horses, which induced us to make such a long day's march, even where we were encamped the country has been overrun by fire, and very little grass left for the horses, hungry and fatigued as they are. Two of the sick men are very ill.

FRIDAY, September 16. Moved five or six miles up the river, and crossed it a little below the fork of Snake River and Salmon River.[173] We got two canoes[174] from the Indians, yet it was near night when the baggage was all across. Some Indians encamped with us. Some horses bought from them, but the people are such fools that they outbid each other and gave double the price they ought for a horse.

SATURDAY, September 17. Marched two and one-half hours, eight miles, up the river[175] to above the forks where we encamped to allow our horses to feed a little as they have had very little these last two nights. Several Indians joined us in the evening.

---

171 Camping on the 14th, near the junction of the Wenaha with the Grande Rounde River. – W. S. L.

172 To Nez Percé or Snake River; the day's march has been down the Grande Rounde and crossing this stream. The camp was made on the banks of the Snake River some distance about south of the mouth of the Grande Rounde. – W. S. L.

173 Mr. Elliott thinks Work should have written "Clearwater."

174 Bancroft MS. reads "candes" or beaver.

175 That is, up on north bank of the Salmon River to near Wapshilla Creek. – W. S. L. Mr. Elliott thinks this should be Clearwater.

SUNDAY, September 18. There being excellent grazing here for the horses we did not move camp in order to allow them to feed. Some more Indians joined us. They had a religious dance. Some horses were traded from them, and others exchanged. One of them made a present of one, and received a present to the value in return.

MONDAY, September 19. Marched four hours, twelve miles E. N. E. up the river,[176] the road in places stony, but otherwise good.

TUESDAY, September 20. Continued our route up the river three hours, ten miles E. N. E. The road the same as yesterday, some stony spots. We encamped in the evening near the chief Sowities lodge. Some rain in the evening.

WEDNESDAY, September 21. Heavy rain in the night and forepart of the day, fine weather afternoon.

The unfavorable weather deterred us from moving camp in the morning. Afterwards we did not start on account of the illness of one of Satrouxs little daughters, who is dying. The chief Sauwashen made us a present of a moose for the people to eat.

THURSDAY, September 22. Fine weather.

Continued our route three hours, ten miles E. N. up the river. A good deal of the road very stony, and bad for the horses feet. We were recommended by some of the Indians to take the road on the opposite side of the river as there were less stones. They advised us to keep to the N. side as it was shorter and leveller. There is all along good grazing for the horses.

FRIDAY, September 23. Stormy, raw, cold weather in the morning, fine afterwards.

---

[176] Camping on north bank of Salmon east of the big bend south of Deep Creek. – W. S. L. Mr. Elliott thinks this should be Clearwater.

Proceeded three and three-fourths hours, eleven miles E.N.E. up the river. The country here becomes more hilly, and the hills approaching close to the river on both sides. Our road the most of the day along the brow of the hill, and was good except a short piece which was stony in the morning.

SATURDAY, September 24. Cold in the morning, but fine weather afterwards.

Continued our journey one and one-half hours, five miles up the river to a fork[177] which falls in from the northward, where we encamped with some Indians as it would have been too long to go to another good encampment. There is plenty of grass for the horses.

SUNDAY, September 25. Continued our journey up the river to where the road leaves the river to strike into the country to Camass Plain.[178] The country hilly and partially wooded.

MONDAY, September 26. Fine weather, but cooler in the morning.

Quitted the river and proceeded across the country five hours, twenty miles E.N.E. to Camass Plains.[179] The road through a woody country, very hilly in the morning but pretty level afterwards. Found some Indians here. It is a great place for collecting camass.

TUESDAY, September 27. Sharp frost in the night,

[177] North fork of Clearwater. – T. C. E.

[178] Along the Lolo Trail. – P. C. P.

[179] These are the North Camas Plains in what is now called the "Camas Prairie country" between the Salmon and Clearwater. There are many "camas" plains or prairies in Idaho, the most important being the "Big Camas Prairie," and the "Little Camas Prairie" in Elmore County, Idaho, along the east branch of the Malade or Big Wood River. There is also a "Little Camas Prairie" on the south side of the Boise River in Elmore County, Idaho. – W. S. L.

Mr. Elliott and Mr. Rees believe this should be north of the Clearwater near Weippe. – P. C .P.

and cooler in the morning, fine weather during the day.

Did not raise camp in order to allow the horses to feed before taking the summits. Some horses were traded from the Indians, and some exchanged. It is very difficult to effect any bargains with them.

WEDNESDAY, September 28. Sharp frost in the night, fine weather afterwards.

Proceeded on our journey five and one-half hours, eighteen miles N.N.E. to a little plain,[180] the greater part of the way through very thick woods and difficult road though well frequented.

THURSDAY, September 29. Frost in the morning, fine weather afterwards.

Did not raise camp owing to one of Satraux children, a little girl, who has been some time ailing dying this morning.

FRIDAY, September 30. Fog and frost in the morning, fine weather afterwards. Proceeded on our journey eight hours, twenty-four miles N.N.E. through continual thick woods and up several steep hills,[181] and encamped in a valley, where there is very little grass for the horses, and very little water.

FRIDAY, September 30. Began to rain a little before daylight, and rained all day. In the evening a great deal of thunder with very heavy rain and hail.

Raised camp and moved one and one-half hours, four miles N.N.E. to a little valley[182] where there is a little grass for the horses. The country here has been burnt and is pretty bare of wood.

---

180 Near Weippe camping probably some place to north and east of Pierce City. – J. E. R.

181 Along Lolo Trail. – J. E. R.

182 Musselshell Creek. – J. E. R.

SATURDAY, October 1. Began to snow in the night, and snowed all day.

The bad weather deterred us from raising camp. M. Plante lost a colt yesterday.

SUNDAY, October 2. Some snow in the morning. Cold weather, the snow thawing. Continued our journey eight and one-half hours, twenty-four miles N.N.N.E. over very steep hills and through thick wood, and encamped later in the evening in a deep valley[183] with little or no grass and nothing but brambles and briars for our horses to feed upon. We let them loose in the night and expect we will be able to find them in the morning as they cannot travel in the [heat?]. Our Indian guide returned for us this morning, we have now fallen on the great road.[184] There is a better place for encamping on the hill behind us, but we did not know it. Two horses gave up on the way. The snow on the hills is about nine inches deep. Both people and horses much fatigued, and completely drenched on arrival at camp. The soft melting snow falling off the trees wet everything.

MONDAY, October 3. Fair weather till towards evening when it began to snow.

Continued our journey four and one-half hours, N.N.E., seventeen miles over steep hills, through thick woods, and encamped later in the evening in a hill the side of which was clear of woods, and where we had the satisfaction of finding a good deal of grass for our horses, though it was covered with snow.[185] By daylight all hands were seeking the horses, the most of

183 Deep Saddle on Weitas Creek. – J. E. R.

184 Lolo Trail. – P. C. P.

185 Bald Mountain. – J. E. R.

them were found sooner than expected [some] of them could not be found during the day though the people went in search of them till late, but the one trusted to the other, and I think did not seek effectually for them.

TUESDAY, October 4. Snowed thick nearly all day, the snow melting a little.

Did not raise camp on account of the bad weather, and to allow the people to seek the stray horses, they were off in quest of them all day, three of them were found. There are still missing seven. . . .

WEDNESDAY, October 5. Snowing most part of the day, the snow melting as it falls.

Continued our route five hours, fifteen miles N. N. E. through thick woods and over some hills, one very steep, and encamped later in a small swamp with scarcely any grass, and that little covered with snow,[186] so that the poor, starving horses could not get at it. Owing to the soft snow falling and the bad weather the people and horses much fatigued. A dismal encampment.

THURSDAY, October 6. Snowed the most of the day.

It was late before the horses were found, and some of them not till the evening. We, nevertheless, raised camp and marched four and one-half hours, twelve miles N. N. E. over a hilly country thickly wooded, and encamped in the evening on the side of a hill clear of woods, and very little snow with a little grass, and herbage scattered thickly over it.[187] Our poor horses will be able to feed a little. A few lodges of the people remained behind to seek the stray horses. . . A horse, belonging to G. Paus, died at the encampment. Some more horses gave up on the way.

186 Indian Grave Camp. – J. E. R.

187 Indian Post Office. – J. E. R.

FRIDAY, October 7. Snowed thick, and cold weather the most of the day.

Proceeded on our journey five and one-half hours, fifteen miles, and encamped where there is a little feeding for the horses on the declivity of a hill where there is a little snow and pretty clear of wood. The people who remained behind came up with the camp. They found all the horses that were astray yesterday, but two cannot be found today. Two of the men, J. Louis and J. Rayburn who went back to a station of the first in quest of the stray horses, but saw nothing of them. The snow on the mountains there is nearly six feet deep, it was with difficulty they could keep the track. We have not yet had the snow a foot deep. The road today lay over hills, one of them very steep, and the road embarrassed with fallen wood.

SATURDAY, October 8. Fair weather.

Continued our journey five and one-half hours, fifteen miles over a succession of hills and down a very steep bank to the river[188] which we left on the [25] September. Here we stopped for the night though we are among the woods, and scarcely any grass for the horses, but we apprehend several of the horses would not be able to get to a little station ahead, but we do not know how far. Here we have no snow. . .

SUNDAY, October 9. Rained in the night and forepart of the day.

Raised camp, and marched two and one-half hours, eight miles up a steep, long hill to a small creek[189] with some swampy clear ground on its banks where there is a good deal of good grass for the horses, of which they

188 Middle fork of the Clearwater. – P. C. P.

189 Pack Creek, across the Bitter Root Divide. – J. E. R.

are in much need. Some of the people remained behind to allow the horses to feed and repose. They said they found a little grass among the hills.

MONDAY, October 10. Rained and a little snow fell in the night and forepart of the day.

The bad weather deterred us from raising camp, moreover, our horses are in much need of feeding. This is a good place. Some of the people who were behind came up, some remain behind still.

TUESDAY, October 11. Very heavy rain all day.

On account of the bad weather we did not raise camp. Though the horses have a good feeding this continual rain is much against them, and a great many of them are very lean.

WEDNESDAY, October 12. Continual rain and sleet in the night and all day.

Did not raise camp. The rest of the people who remained behind came up, they are completely drenched.

THURSDAY, October 13. Overcast, fair weather forepart of the day, rain in the evening.

Raised camp and proceeded three and one-half hours, eleven miles N. to a small plain at hot spring on Saloas River.[190] The road today not hilly but very much embarrassed with fallen wood, and fatiguing on the horses. Three gave up by the way, and three were lost at the

190 *Le Louis* in Bancroft MS. Lolo Hot Springs. From October 2 to October 13. Work's journal states he marched about one hundred miles to Lolo Pass. The line of march was probably along the Lolo Trail and varied from southeast to northeast. October 13 Work states he was thirteen miles south of Lolo Pass. During this march Work's party probably crossed the headwaters of the Clearwater, the South Fork, Selway Fork, Middle Fork to Lolo Pass. Local tradition has it that the name Lolo, for many years spelled Lou Lou, is an Indian pronunciation of Lawrence – the name of a trapper and trader who lived during the fifties on this creek. Judge Franklin Woody, a pioneer of western Montana, and Duncan MacDonald, a half-

encampment and could not be found, and one lost in the wood. The people who are ahead killed fourteen beaver.

FRIDAY, October 14. Light rain in the morning, it then faired a little, but the rain soon came on again and continued all day.

Raised camp and marched five and one-half hours, fifteen miles N. to a little fork which falls in from the westward.[191] The road very hilly and slippery and miry, and exceedingly fatiguing both on the horses and people. Some of the horses gave up on the way owing to the bad road and the bad weather. This was a most harrassing day both on the men and horses. Some of the people were out hunting, but without success. There are a few chiveraux[192] about this plain. Pichette killed a bear.

breed, the son of an old Hudson's Bay Company trader and now tribal judge of the Salish or Flathead Indian tribe, both declared this is the true origin of the word. See Wheeler, *Trail of Lewis and Clark*, ii, 78. – P. C. P.

A more plausible explanation is that the present name of the creek and mountain pass, "Lolo," is a corruption of the French name *Le Louis* given the stream and pass by the fur traders in honor of Meriwether Lewis. – W. S. L.

Jacob A. Meyers states that this word is the Chinook for the verb *pack* or *carry*; and that "Lolo" Pass simply means "pack" pass.

Frederick J. Long, *Dictionary of Chinook Jargon*. Lo-Lo = to carry, 9.

Gill, John, *Dictionary of the Chinook Jargon*, Portland, 1909, 14.

Shaw, George C. *The Chinook Jargon and How to Use It*, Seattle, 1909, 44.

Phillip, W. S. *The Chinook Book*, Seattle, 1913, 108.

Gibbs, George S. *A Dictionary of the Chinook Jargon or Trade Language of Oregon*, Washington, 1863, 34.

Hibben, T. L. *Dictionary of the Chinook Jargon or Indian Trade Language of the Northwest Coast*, Victoria, B.C., 1899, 25.

Hale, Horatio. *An International Idiom, a Manual of the Oregon Trade Language or Chinook Jargon*, London, 1890, 54.

191 Really northeast down Lolo Creek to Grave Creek on the Lewis and Clark trail. – P. C. P.

192 *Cheveraux* = deer.

SATURDAY, October 15. Overcast, showery weather.

Did not raise camp in order to allow the horses to repose a little and feed after the hard day's work yesterday, they are much fatigued. Those that were left behind yesterday were brought up to the camp this morning. Several of the people out hunting. Satoux killed two deer, Gadif one, T. Smith two and Charlie one sheep.

SUNDAY, October 16. Clear, fine, sunny weather.

Did not raise camp in order to allow the horses to feed as there is pretty good grass here, and as we must soon begin night guard. It was, moreover, necessary to dry out things, they are nearly rotten. Some of the horses which were left behind were brought up. A part of the people raised camp and moved a short encampment farther on. Some of the people are out hunting.

MONDAY, October 17. Cloudy, showery weather.

Raised camp and proceeded three hours, nine miles E. N. E.[193] to a nice plain where there is a good feeding for the horses. The men ahead killed beaver and one elk and [sic] two beaver.

TUESDAY, October 18. Cloudy, showery in the afternoon.

Continued our journey six hours, E. N. E. twelve miles down the river to Bitter Root River,[194] the road good. Here we commenced night guard on our horses. Some of the people were hunting, but with little success.

[193] Down Lolo Creek to the neighborhood of Woodman.—P. C. P.

[194] Bitter Root River was so called from the "Spettellum" (Flathead Indian word for the "bitter root" or *Lewisa rediviva*), an important article of Indian food growing in profusion through the Bitter Root valley.—W. S. L. From here Work followed the trail of Lewis on his return down the Bitter Root, up Clark's Fork, and the Blackfoot River.—P. C. P.

WEDNESDAY, October 19. Rained in the night and all day.

Did not raise camp in order to allow the horses to feed, since there is fine grass. Three elk and a moose were killed.

THURSDAY, October 20. Fair weather in the morning, but heavy rain afterward.

Marched one and one-half hours, seven miles E. N. E. across a fine plain to the river at the entrance of Hell's Gates.[195]

FRIDAY, October 21. Snowed the most of the day. The snow melts as it falls.

Raised camp and proceeded up the river N. N. E. two hours, eight miles to the fork of Blackfoot River.[196]

SATURDAY, October 22. Overcast in the morning, thick snow all day afterward.

Proceeded up the Blackfoot River four and one-half hours, fifteen miles N.N. E. and encamped in the woods.[197] The road hilly, and in places stony, thick woods all the way, very little grass for the horses at night.

SUNDAY, October 23. Overcast, mild weather.

Proceeded two hours, eight miles E. across the river and a point of woods to Camass Plain,[198] a fine feeding

---

195 Hell's Gate:—Porte d'enfer of the French fur traders, just east of Missoula, Montana. A defile through the dividing ridges of the mountains, noted as being the great war road by which the Piegan and Blackfoot Indians often visited the west side of the Rockies, and the pass by which the Flatheads and other tribes crossed over to the Missouri side in quest of buffalo, and the scene of many a bloody contest between these hostile nations. It was the usual and only well known place to the whites for passing the mountains in this vicinity. See Ross, *Fur Hunters*, ii, 12-13.—W. S. L. Clark's Fork of the Columbia flows through this defile.—P. C. P.

196 That is mouth of the Blackfoot River.—W. S. L.

197 Near McNamara's Landing.—H. F. HERMAN.

198 Near Potomac.—H. F. H. There is a Camas Plain at this place—P. C. P.

THE BLACKFOOT RIVER, NEAR MCNAMARA'S LANDING
Work's party encamped here, October 22, 1831. This valley had long been a battle-ground between the Blackfoot and Flathead Indians.

place for the horses. The road good. The hail which fell yesterday nearly all melted. Late in the evening P. Finlay and an Indian arrived from the Flathead camp which they left yesterday on Bitter Root River. From these people we learn that a large party of Americans are hunting in the grounds which we are going to, that they have hunted during the summer several branches of the Missouri which we intended to visit, besides some other forks.[199] A large party are also wintering on Salvos [Salmon] River.[200] Three or four beaver were killed.

MONDAY, October 24. Raw, cold weather, snow showers, sharp frost in the night.

Moved camp and marched two and one-half hours, eight miles N. E. through woods to a plain,[201] the road good, good feeding for the horses. One elk, a beaver and a bear were killed. The people who arrived yesterday returned. Four of our people, A. Finlay, M. Finlay, M. Plante, and A. Plante,[202] quit the party and returned with them, contrary to my wish. These men are half Indians, and so whimsical that they cannot be relied more upon than Indians. Leaving me thus and weakening the party in a dangerous country is rascally conduct, they had promised to remain with the party two years. They are too lazy to keep watch. Beaver were taken.

TUESDAY, October 25. Frost in the night, raw, cold weather and much snow in the middle of the day.

Raised camp and marched two hours, seven miles N.

---

199 See The Fur Trade in the Northwest for account of American fur trade in this region.

200 Bancroft MS. reads "Salmon."

201 Near Sunset Hill. – H. F. H.

202 See p. 64.

across the river to a small fork[203] at a good feeding place for the horses. The people out with their traps, six beaver taken. Payette killed a black-tailed deer and Smith two bears.

WEDNESDAY, October 26. Overcast weather, some light snow.

Did not raise camp in order to make lodge poles, all hands busily employed providing themselves with ones. Some of the men who slept out last night arrived, one, old Bairvent, is still behind. Beaver taken. Kanota killed an elk.

THURSDAY, October 27. Snowed all day.

The unfavorable weather deterred us from raising camp. Two beaver were taken. The snow melted early as it fell. No news yet of Baisvent. . .

FRIDAY, October 28. Snowed all day, snow melted nearly as soon as it fell.

Raised camp, and proceeded up the river three and one-half hours, twelve miles E. S. E.[204] We missed the road, and passed through a bad part of the woods. Sent a party of men in quest of Bainvent. They found him where his traps were set, he was lost, and so bewildered that he did not know where to go. The old F. H. chief, LaBent, accompanied by his son, a boy, arrived late in the evening in order to accompany us. He left his people yesterday. Eighteen beaver were taken. Some of the people were in quest of elk, only one was killed by Sotraux.

SATURDAY, October 29. Stormy, cold weather, hail and snow showers.

203 Mouth of Clearwater. – H. F. H.

204 Should be E. N. E. Camping on Cottonwood Creek. – H. F. H. See note 167 regarding Work's compass directions.

Moved one hour, four miles E. S. E. up the river to a fork which falls in from the northward.[205] Twelve beaver and two otter were taken. Some of the hunters were out and killed two elk. Some marks of the Americans were seen. The Indians had hunted the little forks up this far, and probably all above this is hunted by Americans, so that nothing is left for us.

SUNDAY, October 30. Overcast, cold weather.

Proceeded one and one-half hours, six miles E. S. E. across a point to another fork of the river which falls in from the N. E.,[206] and here, as well as in the other two forks there has been a good many beaver, but recently hunted by the Americans. Some beaver still remain, but they are shy and difficult to take. This fork passes through a mountain at no great distance, the head of it beyond the mountain which is in a plain country, is said to be rich in beaver, but it is in the Blackfoot country and very dangerous, and at this late season frozen, so that it could not be traded. The small streams are all getting frozen up. The people proceeded up the fork with the traps to near the [. . .] lies through a narrow valley thickly wooded with steep hills on each side. No marks of Blackfeet are to be seen, but an old guide, LaBruh [La Buche] warned the people to be particularly on their guard as that was their road and their country not far off. Thirteen beaver were taken.

MONDAY, October 31. Cloudy, fine weather.

Did not raise camp in order to allow the people time to try what success there might be with the traps, which they set yesterday. The men are off in different direc-

205 Monteur Creek. – H. F. H. Named after Nicholas Monteur, a Northwest Company clerk, associated with David Thompson and one of the first white men in the Kootenai River district of Montana. – W. S. L.

206 A small creek near Ovando. – H. F. H.

tions visiting the traps and hunting. Before noon Champagne, Masson and C. Riendeau arrived with the news that some of their traps had been stolen by the Blackfeet and that they suspected J. Cloutier was killed as three shots were fired (we heard the shots here) very shortly after he passed them, two other men A. Letandre and Curry who were still farther up the river, it is feared were also killed. Our cannon was fired twice to apprise our men who were out of the enemy's approach,[207] and a party accompanied by old La Buche and Soteau, were immediately sent off but on entering the valley they heard some of our people firing at ducks below the camp, and imagining that perhaps it was the enemy approaching the camp in that direction returned with one of the men (Carney) who had from his swiftness outrun the savages and barely escaped with his life, he relates that he and Letandre were both visiting a trap, had left their horses on the bank and set their arms beside them, when they heard the shots fired at Cloutier, when one proposed to the other to be off, but were instantly fired upon by five or six of the savages from the bank, poor Letandre was wounded but they missed C[arney] who crossed the river and escaped to the mountains, both were taken so suddenly that they had not time or wanted presence of mind to fly to their arms. C[arney] thinks he saw only six Indians. A party of fifteen men accompanied by Payette, La Buche and Soteau, immediately went off to visit the place and found Cloutier and Letandre both dead, the former

[207] Bancroft MS. here inserts:

J. Clantin 6 traps stolen 4 remaining
J. Covine 3 do. do. & 1 do.
F. Letande 3 " "
C. Rondeau 1 do. do. – P. C. P.

stripped of his clothes, neither of them were scalped or mangled, except that wolves or Indian dogs had devoured one of Cloutier's thighs, he seems to have been killed instantly, both of his arms were broken below the shoulders and the balls passed through his breast, the savages were so near that from the size and appearance of the wounds the wadding as well as the balls appear to have entered his body. Letandre seems not to have died so soon, he received two balls one passed through his left breast near his heart, and one through his back and belly, besides a knife was dashed into his head at the root of his nose, probably to dispatch him. They did not take his waistcoat or shirt. The party is not supposed to have been more than ten or twelve men in all, after committing the murder they seem to have made a most precipitate retreat as they threw away two robes, a pair of leggins, several cords, and two of the traps which they had stolen. They have, however, got three horses, three guns, and horse bags, and ammunition of two men, and traps from Cloutier, Letandre, Carney, Cloutier's traps were all on his horse as he had not set any. Champagne [Carney?] apprised Cloutier that his traps had been stolen and advised him to take care of himself, he replied yes take care of yourselves and pushed on without stopping and was in a few minutes afterwards killed. The party are supposed to have come from below, they had dogs with them.

TUESDAY, November 1. Cold, stormy weather.

Did not raise camp on account of it being All Saint's Day which is a great festival with the [Fr.] Canadians. Buried the remains of our unfortunates who came to such an untimely end yesterday by the hands of the inhuman, murderous Blackfeet.

WEDNESDAY [November] 2. Cloudy, fine weather.

Raised camp and proceeded three and one-half hours, fourteen miles E. S. E. across a point to another fork and up it to near the upper end of a narrow defile, through which this fork here runs,[208] which is partially wooded. The people visited their traps, twenty-one beaver were taken. Beaver have been numerous here some time ago, but it has recently been hunted by the Americans, there are still some bear [beaver] here, but they are very shy and difficult to take. The swamps and small rivulets where beaver are to be found are freezing up so that the beaver cannot be taken. Kanota's horse was shot by his Indian last night.

THURSDAY [November] 3. Raw, cold weather.

Marched two and one-fourth hours, nine miles E. S. E. up the river and across a point to a small swamp where we encamped, here this fork issues from the mountain from the northward.[209] The people visited the river but no chance of taking any beaver, it has been so recently hunted by the Americans.

FRIDAY [November] 4. Raw, cold weather, some hail showers in the morning.

Marched three and one-fourth hours, fourteen miles E. S. E. to the Little Blackfoot River, where we encamped on a small point surrounded by hills.[210] Some of the people set a few traps. Some buffalo bulls were observed on the hills, a party of the people went after them and killed two. The meat is very indifferent, but nevertheless acceptable as provisions are very scarce with us.

---

208 Up Nevada Creek to mouth of Cottonwood Creek, near the present town of Helmville. – H. F. H.

209 Back to Nevada Creek. – H. F. H.

210 Near the present Avon.

SATURDAY [November] 5. Overcast, cold weather. Marched three hours, twelve miles S. S. E. down the river and across a point to [Flint?] River,[211] where we encamped, here is good feeding for the horses. A bull was killed but notwithstanding the people had little to eat; none of the meat was taken.

SUNDAY [November] 6. Cloudy, blowing, fresh, some rain in the evening.

Marched two and one-half hours, eight miles S. S. W. up the river[212] and some of the people set a few traps, little signs of beaver. The Americans hunted here in the summer. The people were out hunting but very little success. They thought two days ago that bulls would be found everywhere, but they are disappointed.

MONDAY [November] 7. Cloudy, fine, mild weather.

Marched one and one-half hours, six miles S. S. W. up the river, and camped on a fork which falls in from the westward,[213] here there is excellent feeding for the horses. The people set their traps – one beaver taken. This river was formerly rich, but being frequently hunted both by the whites and the Indians, beaver now are very scarce in it. The people were out hunting but only a bull and a sheep were killed. Provisions are becoming scarce with us.

---

[211] Bancroft MS. reads "Flint." The party could not have arrived at Flint Creek from the Little Blackfoot in so short a time. Probably Deer Lodge River, a local name for a part of Clark's Fork as indicated by Work's later travels. – P. C. P.

According to Angus McDonald the first gold found in Montana was discovered near Flint Creek in 1850. See McDonald's *A Few Items of the West.* In Washington Historical Society *Quarterly*, viii, 188-229. – W. S. L.

The first real discovery of gold was on Gold Creek about twenty miles east. – P. C. P.

[212] Should be S. S. E. to near Deer Lodge. – P. C. P.

[213] Probably Dempsey Creek. – P. C. P.

TUESDAY [November] 8. Overcast, foggy, cold weather, rained heavy the forepart of the night and afterwards snowed, near half a foot of snow fell.

Did not raise camp in order to allow the people to try what success they might have with their traps, and that they might endeavor to kill some bulls for food. Several of the people went out hunting.

WEDNESDAY [November] 9. Cloudy, cold weather. Marched two and one-fourth hours, eight miles S. S. E. up the river to the hot spring.[214] The road good through a fine plain. The men visited their traps which had been in the water two nights, twenty-one beaver were taken. Notwithstanding, that this quarter has been recently hunted both by the Indians and Americans, there are still some beaver, but having been so lately hunted they are very shy, moreover the dams and small forks are freezing up so that they cannot be taken. Several of the people were in the mountains hunting sheep, and killed five.

THURSDAY [November] 10. Raw, cold weather, froze keen in the night.

Marched two hours, eight miles S. S. E. up the river, here we had to leave it and cross a small hill [215] to the waters of the Missouri.[216] Several of the people out hunting. Numbers of bulls were seen ahead. No beaver taken in the traps which were set yesterday, they were frozen up.

FRIDAY [November] 11. Raw, cold weather.

Marched S. S. E. four hours, fifteen miles S. S. E. to a

[214] Warm Springs, Montana. – P. C. P.

[215] Up Clark's Fork and Silver Bow Creek to near Stuart, Montana. Crossed over Deer Lodge Pass, now used by the Oregon Short Line. – JEAN BISHOP.

[216] One of the small creeks tributary to the Big Hole River. – P. C. P.

small branch of the Missouri.[217] This was a fatiguing day both to horses and people, but there was no place to camp nearer. Several bulls were seen, the people killed some of them, it was difficult to deter them from rising them, though it may raise them and be the means of raising the buffalo ahead.

SATURDAY [November] 12. Weather milder than these days past.

Marched three hours, eleven miles S. S. E. to the river of the Grand Toux[218] where it receives the small river on which we were encamped last night. Some herds of bulls were seen feeding on the hills on both sides of the road, the people prevented from going after them and they remained undisturbed. From the appearance of the tracks the bulls which were raised yesterday have gone on ahead and taken some cows that were near this place with them. From a hill numbers of buffalo were seen in the plain ahead of us.

SUNDAY [November] 13. Cloudy, mild weather. It was very cold last night, and the river was driving full of ice this morning, and the small streams are nearly all frozen over.

Marched ten miles, three hours S. E. across a range of hills and down the river on which we were encamped yesterday,[219] and stopped at the plain where the buffalo were seen yesterday, but the grand band were all gone, there are however a number of bulls remaining and

[217] Head of Divide Creek. – J. B.

[218] Bancroft MS. reads "Grand Horse." Big Hole, or Wisdom River. – P. C. P. Called by the French Canadian trappers *Le Grand Trou*, meaning "big hole," from which the valley and the river took its name. – W. S. L.

[219] Ten miles across hills to mouth of Camp Creek on the Big Hole River near Melrose. At the present time the road crosses these hills to avoid a canyon of the Big Hole. This river opens out into a "plain" at Melrose. – J. B.

some cows among them, whom the people went after and killed eight or ten of them, but the most of them were very lean.

MONDAY [November] 14. Cloudy, cold weather.

Marched one and one-half hours, five miles S.E. down the river, and encamped to allow the horses to feed where there is some grass, left by the buffalo. About this part of the river there were formerly a good many beaver and our guide says there are a few yet but on account of the coldness and the sides of the river being frozen, they cannot be taken now. Shortly after we encamped, Soteau who had gone to the hills, brought a large herd of buffalo close by the camp. Several of the people immediately went after them and killed eight or ten of them.

TUESDAY [November] 15. Overcast, cold, stormy weather.

Did not raise camp in order to allow the horses to feed of which they are in very great need, for some time past the grass has been both scarce and indifferent, and the horses having to be confined at night without eating, they are becoming very poor.

WEDNESDAY [November] 16. Weather as yesterday.

Proceeded on our journey two and one-half hours, eight miles S.S.E. to a small creek[220] which falls into the river which we left this morning. No buffalo to be seen on the road, but some of the men who went to the hills saw plenty ahead.

THURSDAY [November] 17. Froze keen in the night; overcast, cold weather during the day.

[220] Five miles below Melrose to a tributary called Birch Creek. From Birch Creek the party could see a large part of the Beaverhead valley where there were "plenty" of buffalo. – J. B.

Beaverhead Rock

[See Footnote 221]

Moved camp and marched three and one-half hours, nine miles S. S. E. over sandy hills to an extensive plain on the Missouri where we encamped a little above the Beaverhead,[221] here the plains on both sides of the river are covered with large herds of buffalo, the most of the people went after them and killed twenty-four cows; some of them very fat. The river here is frozen, a small channel on which we are encamped is frozen over, and though the ground is low there is some snow along the river.

FRIDAY [November] 18. Overcast, cold weather, stormy towards evening.

Did not raise camp in order to allow our horses to feed, there is good grass here, and to afford the people time to kill more meat and dry it. Several of the people were out hunting and killed fifteen buffalo. Some of the men saw three Indians on horseback which they supposed to be Blackfeet, it was too late when the peo-

[221] Nine miles S. S. E. must be S. S. W. Beaverhead:–Beaverhead Rock on the Beaverhead River, below Dillon, an Indian name, used by Lewis and Clark.–P. C. P. "August 10, Saturday, 1805. We proceeded on passed a remarkable clift point on the star'd side about one hundred and fifty feet high, this clift the Indians call the Beaver's head, opposite at three hundred yards is a low clift of fifty feet which is a spur of the mountain on the star'd about four miles." Thwaites, [ed.] *Original Journals of Lewis & Clark*, ii, 328.

"Near Lovell's, in Beaverhead valley, and in full view of the stage road, is Beaverhead Rock. It is this quaint landmark which gives river, valley, and county their name; and as there is very good likeness of it in these pages, readers will unite in saying that the title is appropriately bestowed. The rock rises three hundred feet above the river, and is so near the perpendicular that a plummet suspended from its summit would drop into the edge of the deep eddy which washes its southern base. A short walk up the canyon, bursting from the cliffs by the roadside, is a cluster of warm springs. They throw off a strong stream of water, and, dropping from a ledge some twenty-five feet above the road, form the pretty little Twin Falls, which Montana-bound people admire so much." Strahorn (Robert E.), *To the Rockies and Beyond*, Omaha, 1879, 178.

ple arrived from the buffalo hunt to send to examine the tracks and to ascertain the number of the party. We are here just in the road of the Blackfeet.

SATURDAY [November] 19. Blew a storm from the southward, though the weather is cold the snow thawed a little.

Did not raise camp, some of the people went after buffalo but with little success, the stormy weather was unfavorable for hunting. Our guide Buche, and some men went to examine the Indian tracks which were seen yesterday, they compute the party to consist of twenty or twenty-three men, they have three horses with them and are going down the river, they passed on the opposite side in the night.

SUNDAY [November] 20. Cold, stormy weather.

Proceeded up the river two and three-fourths hours, ten miles S. and crossed the river.[222] No buffalo to be seen at our first station, but near our first encampment there are several herds, the people went after them and killed several. Tracks of Blackfeet are here in the snow.

MONDAY [November] 21. Cloudy, cold weather.

Did not raise camp as we have good feeding for the horses and there are buffalo close by. There is little necessity for our hurrying on as the danger from the Blackfeet is the same wherever we can go. F. Payette is very ill, and unable to sit on a horse. The people went a-hunting and killed several buffalo.

TUESDAY [November] 22. Cloudy, cold weather but milder than these days past.

Did not raise camp in order to allow the horses to feed and that the people might have time to dry their

[222] Up Beaverhead River to near Dillon. — P. C. P.

meat. Some of the people went after buffalo and killed only five.

WEDNESDAY [November] 23. Stormy weather, snowing and drifting forepart of the day.

The unfavorable weather deterred us from raising camp as we intended. No buffalo to be seen in our neighborhood.

THURSDAY [November] 24. Cloudy, cold weather some light snow and blowing towards evening.

During the second watch about six o'clock last night a party of Blackfeet approached the camp and fired upon the men who were guarding the horses about fifty yards from the lodges, at the same time raising a hideous war yell to frighten the horses which it did and they ran off but were fortunately soon stopped and brought back chiefly by the activity of Champagne who was one of the men on watch. In the meantime the Indians continued firing upon the lodges and on our people who turned about to the plains to meet them. Our cannon was fired in the direction some of them were supposed to be in, they ceased firing immediately and made off. Not knowing the strength of the party and the party being occupied securing the horses they were not pursued. Unfortunately J. Desland, one of the men on guard, was dangerously if not mortally wounded by the first fire from the savages, the ball entered his left breast and came out under his left arm, one of the ribs and part of the breast bone supposed to be broken, he was one of the men on guard nearest the bushes where the villians concealed themselves, he is very ill today and too weak to be moved which deterred us from raising camp. On visiting their tracks this morning the party is supposed not to have exceeded twenty men. It is to be regretted it was not daylight as probably few of the daring scoundrels would have escaped. They threw away several cords and other things in their hurry to be off, one of the cords is a strand of a tarred [tanned?] boat line.

FRIDAY [November] 25. Cloudy, mild weather.

The wounded men being too ill to be moved we did not move camp. We have still good grass here for the horses, but having them up at night this cold weather and being fourteen or fifteen hours without eating is very hard upon them, yet we can't do otherwise as we know not when a band of Blackfeet may set upon us. No buffalo to be seen.

SATURDAY [November] 26. Stormy, cold weather.

Moved camp and marched three hours S. S. W., ten miles up the river and encamped on a small plain; here the rocks approach close to the river on both sides.[223] It is not a good situation but we could not find grass in a better. A small band of buffalo were seen, and one or two of them were killed. The wounded man was carried on men's shoulders on a bed constructed on poles, where he lay pretty easy.

SUNDAY [November] 27. Cloudy, cold weather.

Proceeded up the river two hours, seven miles S. S. W. and encamped in a good situation for defence. No buffalo except a chance bull to be seen. The most part of yesterday and today's journey there is a little more snow on the ground than below.

MONDAY [November] 28. Cold weather.

Did not raise camp on account of the wounded man, he requires a little repose. No buffalo except a chance bull to be seen.

[223] Near Barratt's.—P. C. P.

TUESDAY [November] 29. Cloudy, milder weather, than these days past.

Proceeded up the river two and one-half hours, seven miles S. S. W. to the fork of the river.[224] Here the main river falls from the eastward and the horse plain fork comes from the S. S. W. We have no wood here but willows, so that notwithstanding the cold weather we cannot keep large fires. Large herds of buffalo were found feeding here, the people immediately went in pursuit of them and killed upwards of twenty. The wounded man complains of being ill.

WEDNESDAY [November] 30. Stormy, cold weather, some hail showers in the evening.

Did not raise camp principally on account of the wounded man, and to allow the people to dry the meat which was killed yesterday. We have good feeding here for the horses. The people went after buffalo, but the dogs had raised them and they could not be come up with. Hardly one is now to be seen.

THURSDAY, December 1. Stormy, cold weather.

Proceeded three hours, ten miles S. S. W. up the river and encamped in a tuft of willows, where we had no wood but some small willows and wormwood to warm us.[225] We have good feeding for the horses, in a fine valley. There is no snow on the ground but the river is frozen over. The people went in pursuit of buffalo of which there [are] large bands all around us, and killed a few, our horses are very lean, and few of them able to catch the buffalo now.

[224] Forks of Beaverhead formed by Horse Prairie Creek and Red Rock Creek near Armstead, Montana. Horse Prairie Creek was known to the fur traders by that name. – P. C. P.

[225] Up Horse Prairie Creek to Shoshone Cove named by Lewis and Clark. – J. E. R.

FRIDAY [December] 2. Again stormy weather.

Did not raise camp. The people hunting buffalo and killed a few.

SATURDAY [December] 3. Stormy and very cold all day.

Did not raise camp. Notwithstanding the coldness of the weather, some of the people went after buffalo, but with little success. Our old guide La Buche accompanied by F. Payette, Longtim, Pichette, Quintall and Carney, went up the river on discovery, and observed two Blackfoot Indians passing with four horses, they immediately pursued them, but were not able to come up with them, they have pressed them so hard that they abandoned two of the horses, which our people brought to camp, one of them is known as a Nez Percé horse. Soteau observed another party of Blackfeet with seven horses passing along the mountains some distance from the camp, had he given notice in time, they might have been pursued and killed or at least the horses taken from them. These horses are all supposed to have been stolen from the Nez Percé and F[lat]heads at Salmon River.

SUNDAY [December] 4. Cloudy, cold weather. Fell about three inches of snow in the night.

Several of the people went in quest of buffalo, but killed very few.

MONDAY [December] 5. Stormy, cold weather.

Did not raise camp. Some of the people hunting buffalo, but few were killed. All hands employed themselves cutting grass to give the horses in the night while tied up, which is great service to them.

TUESDAY [December] 6. Cloudy weather, some light snow.

Did not raise camp. The people hunting buffalo.

WEDNESDAY [December] 7. Weather as yesterday.

Some of the people in pursuit of buffalo, but with little success. The most of our runners are so weak that they cannot come up with the buffalo. The ground is so slippery that the horses are afraid.

THURSDAY [December] 8. Mild weather in the morning but became stormy and very cold afterwards.

Raised camp and moved up the river three hours, nine miles S.W. to a steep rock called "Cumcarny" [Cumcarney][226]—previous to reaching the encampment, a large herd of buffalo were observed close to, and the people went after them but killed only two. J. Desland, the wounded man, insisted on going on horseback alone, it is to be feared it will injure him. He is recovering very slowly, and is becoming so peevish tempered that the people who attend him can scarcely bear him. Two Blackfeet with four horses passed yesterday.

FRIDAY [December] 9. Cold, cloudy weather.

Did not raise camp on account of Souteau supposing to have seen some Blackfeet passing with a band of horses, and the people went after them but it turned out that the old man was mistaken.

SATURDAY [December] 10. Cloudy, still, cold weather.

Proceeded two and one-half hours, seven miles S.W. up the middle fork[227] of the river to near the mountain,

[226] This is a Shoshone Indian name, pronounced Coon-carny, and means "campfire," so named on August 16, 1805, because Captain Lewis and Indians built camp to cook breakfast. It is at the narrows, near Brenner.—J. E. R.

[227] Bloody Dick Creek, named for Dick Greene, an Englishman with whom it was always, "bloody this and bloody that."—J. E. R.

and encamped at a hummock of woods at a good place for defence.

SUNDAY [December] 11. Cloudy, cold weather, a bitter cold night.

Early in the morning some Blackfeet were observed ascending the hill opposite our camp; a party of the people immediately went in pursuit of them and they fled and took shelter among thick willows and underwood on the south fork of the river. Our people commenced an attack upon them and continued their fire till late in the evening, when they gave up the attack deeming it too great a risk to go into the wood after them. They conjecture that there were eight or ten Indians, they had eight horses with them which they stole in the night from F[lat]heads on Salmon River. Our people killed three of the horses, and they suppose that two or three of the Indians are badly wounded if not killed, at first they returned a brisk fire on our people, but soon stopped, and lay quiet in their holes, it is probable they had little ammunition. They at first talked with our people, and told them that the F[lat]-heads were close too, and that the Americans had a fort on the Missouri about the forks.[228] They said they did not care to fight with us and enquired why we fired upon them.

MONDAY [December] 12. Some snow in the night, and light snow and sleet during the day. Some of the young men visited the place where the Blackfeet took refuge yesterday. From the appearance of the tracks and blood on the snow they think two at least of the

[228] Fort Union at mouth of Yellowstone. – J. E. R. See The Fur Trade in the Northwest, pp. 30 to 47, for account of American activities.

Indians were killed or very badly wounded, they had concealed themselves in old beaver dams.

TUESDAY [December] 13. A very stormy night with some light snow; light snow during the day.

Some Blackfeet passed with horses, but from the snow and drift, how many could not be ascertained. Two men with two horses passed in the morning, some of them left a mare which our people found; it is known to belong to the F[lat]heads.

WEDNESDAY [December] 14. Very cold and stormy in the night. Moderate in the morning but stormy and very cold afterwards.

Raised camp and proceeded two hours, seven miles S.W. across a point and then up a small fork[229] to near the height of land on the way to Salmon[230] River, where we encamped to be more out of the way of Blackfeet, and be enabled to let our horses feed a little. The snow here is more than a foot deep, and in places drifted to two or three feet deep. A herd of some hundreds of elk were feeding a little to the one side of our camp; some of the people went in pursuit and killed three of them, they are very lean. For the first time since the Blackfeet attacked us we did not tie up our horses.

THURSDAY [December] 15. Stormy and very cold towards midday but mild towards evening.

Raised camp and marched two and three-fourths hours, eight miles S.W. over the height of land and down a small fork of Salmon River.[231] The snow on the height of land more than two feet deep. The road

229 Up Trail Creek. – J. E. R.

230 Salmon River should be Lemhi. – J. E. R.

231 Over Lemhi Pass down Agency Creek to Lemhi River near Tendoy, Idaho. – J. E. R.

most of the day along the side of a slanting hill was slippery and very hard and fatiguing on the horses.

FRIDAY [December] 16. Overcast, milder weather these three days past.

Continued our route two and one-half hours, eight miles S.W. down the creek and across a point to Salmon River. The road, the forepart of the day the same as yesterday but the snow diminished as we descended the river where there is very little. Here we came up with a camp – thirty-eight lodges, F[lat]head Indians, who are ascending the river. They inform us that a large party of Americans are encamped at the fork below,[232] that the Nez Percés with some more Americans have gone up another fork of Salmon River.[233] There is no buffalo below here, and the people both whites and Indians have been short of food for sometime. Here we expect to find buffalo a little farther up the river. A large herd of elk were seen in the mountain near our

[232] The height of land at the sources of the Missouri, the Colorado and the Clark (Pend d'Oreille) and Lewis (Snake) branches of the Columbia was a paradise for the early fur hunters. Manuel Lisa and Andrew Henry of the Missouri Fur Company had been active in this region and Henry had erected a small establishment consisting of several log huts, and known as Henry's post or fort, on Henry's Fork, one of the sources of the Snake River, in January, 1810, a year before the Astor overland party under Mr. Hunt traversed the same section (1810-1811) having as guides Robinson, Renzer, and Hobach, three of Henry's former employees at Henry's post. Sublette, Smith, and Co. had invaded the region in the twenties and many employees of the Rocky Mountain Fur Company, American Fur Company, and many independent traders and trappers were now scattered through the region. Their presence led to the establishment of the great "'American rendezvous" of the trappers of this district. Alexander Ross in 1824, eight years before our author's present writing, complains of the Americans in this region. – W. S. L. The Americans were apparently camped at the junction of the Salmon and Lemhi Rivers. See page 37.

[233] North Fork of the Salmon, as the Nez Percé trail went that way. – J. E. R.

Lewis and Clark Trail over Lemhi Pass
John Work's party passed over this trail on December 15, 1831. The trail was remarkable for its steepness, but was much used by hunters and traders during the fur trading period.

camp this morning. The F[lat]heads killed two Blackfeet horse thieves a few days ago.

SATURDAY [December] 17. Overcast, mild weather.

Did not raise camp in order to allow our horses to feed and repose a little.

SUNDAY [December] 18. Cloudy but rather cold weather.

Did not raise camp. Though some of our people are short of food. The Indians are also short of food.

MONDAY [December] 19. Sharp frost in the night, mild weather during the day.

Raised camp and proceeded two and one-half hours, eight miles S. E. up the river in company with the Indians, and encamped on a fine feeding place for the horses.[234]

TUESDAY [December] 20. Foggy with keen frost in the night and forepart of the day.

Did not raise camp, in order to allow our horses to feed. The most of the Indians moved on ahead, they are starving, it being some time since they saw any buffalo.

WEDNESDAY [December] 21. Weather as yesterday.

Moved up the river two hours, seven miles S. E. to where the Indians are encamped,[235] a good feeding place for the horses. A party of seven American trappers arrived from their camp at the forks below in the evening.

THURSDAY [December] 22. Snowed a little in the night, overcast mild weather during the day.

Did not raise camp. The people traded fifteen beaver from the Americans who went off.

---

[234] Near mouth of Hayden Creek. – J. E. R.

[235] To Mill Creek. – J. E. R.

FRIDAY, December 23. Stormy, cold weather.

Did not raise camp on account of one of the Indians being in a dying state.

SATURDAY [December] 24. Stormy, cold weather.

Moved up the river two and one-half hours, seven miles S. E., and put ashore for the night.[236] The Indians killed a few bulls of which they are in much need as they are starving.

SUNDAY [December] 25. Stormy, cold weather.

Being Christmas Day we did not raise camp. Owing to our not having fallen in with buffalo lately many of the people fared but indifferently having only dry meat, and several of them not much of that.

MONDAY [December] 26. The weather milder than these days past.

Moved camp, and proceeded two hours, seven miles E.[237] to a little fork issuing from the mountains, some buffalo were observed in the morning a good way ahead, several of the Indians and some of our people went in pursuit. They were all bulls. Several of them were killed, our people killed seven of them.

SUNDAY [Tuesday] [December] 27. Mild, soft weather.

Did not raise camp. Some of the Indians went in pursuit of buffalo, and killed a few bulls. Some buffalo supposed to be cows were seen passing over the height of land towards this way in the evening.

WEDNESDAY [December] 28. Mild weather.

Did not raise camp. A herd of buffalo were observed in the morning, the Indians and several of our

236 Eight Mile Creek. – J. E. R.

237 Timber Creek, near Leadore, Idaho. – J. E. R.

people went in pursuit and killed a great many of them. Our people killed seven.

THURSDAY [December] 29. Soft, mild weather.

Raised camp and moved two hours, seven miles S.E. along the foot of the mountains to another small creek.[238] There were some buffalo near but were raised and went off back. Late in the evening the Indians thought they saw two Blackfeet about the camp.

FRIDAY [December] 30. Mild, soft weather.

A few buffalo were to be seen in the morning but they were too far off to go after them; a few Indians went, but killed very few. Some more were seen approaching towards evening. A party of twelve Americans passed in the morning on the way to buffalo. They appeared to be very hungry but did not stop, or they would have received [been asked] to eat from [by] our people, indeed it was not known that they were so short of food till they were gone.

SATURDAY [December] 31. Fine, mild weather.

Nearly all the people with the Indians were out hunting buffalo, and were successful all having killed [?]. Our people killed [?].

SUNDAY [January] 1, 1832. Fine, mild weather.

This being Sunday, and New Years Day neither our people nor the Indians went in pursuit of buffalo tho' large herds were to be seen far off. The men and some of the principal Indians were treated with a dram and some cakes in the morning, and a small quantity of rum had been brought from the fort for the occasion. One of the Americans who passed on Friday returned yesterday evening.

[238] Eighteen Mile Creek. – J. E. R.

MONDAY [January] 2. Stormy the after part of the day but not cold.

Raised camp and moved five miles down the river[239] to find better feeding for our horses, and here it is little better than where we left. Our horses are becoming lean since we came so close to the mountains as the grass tho' of a good quality so thin that they cannot fill their bellies during the day, and don't eat at all during the night. It is apprehended that were we camped on the river in the middle of the valley where there is plenty of long grass, and where our horses would be much better off, that the smoke of the camp would drive off the buffalo to such a distance that we could not get them. So that we must endeavor to kill some provisions, and then feed our horses. Several of the people as well as the Indians went in pursuit of buffalo but the cattle being raised while the hunters were still at too great a distance, and the weather being unfavorable very few were killed, either by the whites or by the Indians and the horses fatigued to little purpose tho' they are from their poverty ill able to bear it. Some of the people saw a camp of Nez Percés who came across the mountains from another fork of Salmon River.[240]

TUESDAY [January] 3. Some light snow.

Some of the people went in pursuit of buffalo. Four chiefs of the Nez Percés paid us a visit. Their camp of twenty-five to thirty lodges is in the opposite side of the valley.

WEDNESDAY [January] 4. Raw, cold weather part of the day.

---

239 Canyon Creek. – J. E. R.

240 Over the Lemhi range by the Eight Mile Trail from Pahsimaroi, a Shoshone word meaning "a lone cedar on the bank of a stream." – J. E. R.

Raised camp and proceeded two hours, seven miles N. to a little way in a cut in the mountains to Cumvarny.[241] The tracks of a horse and a mule supposed to have been stolen from the Americans by the Blackfeet passed through the defile. Some of the young Indians went in pursuit, and would have come up with them had the chief not directed them not to pass a certain place lest they would raise the buffalo.

THURSDAY [January] 5. Some light snow in the morning; fine weather afterwards.

Proceeded three hours, eleven miles N. up the defile and across the height of land to a small fork of the Missouri.[242] Here there is excellent feeding for the horses, and very little snow, tho' in the mountains it was more than two feet deep in places.

FRIDAY [January] 6. Mild, soft weather.

Did not raise camp in order to allow the horses to feed, of which they are in much want.

SATURDAY [January] 7. Light snow the forepart of the day which deterred us from raising camp. The horses have much need of feeding.

SUNDAY [January] 8. Raw, cold weather after part of the day.

Raised camp and proceeded three hours, ten miles N. down the river, here there is good feeding for the horses. Not a buffalo to be seen, though there are the marks of their having been very numerous here not long since. One of my best pack horses was completely disabled by cutting his foot severely with an axe.

MONDAY [January] 9. Cloudy, stormy weather, snow in the morning.

---

[241] Bannack Pass, through which the Gilmore and Pittsburgh railway passes. – P. C. P.

[242] Headwaters of Horse Prairie Creek. – P. C. P.

Continued our journey two and one-half hours, seven miles N. N. E. down the river to below our encampment of the 8 December.[243] No buffalo except a few bulls to be seen though they have been very numerous along here not long since. Some young men were ahead on discovery, and report that they saw some buffalo, and also a party of Blackfeet towards the mountains.

TUESDAY [January] 10. Cold weather in the night and morning and mild afterwards.

Proceeded down the river to the Rock[244] where we arrived about noon after two and one-half hours march, seven miles. Here some of the young men who were ahead of the camp met a party of twenty or twenty-five Blackfeet. A fire was immediately opened on both sides, two of the F[lat]heads were wounded, one in the breast and one in the thumb. On some more of our party coming up, the Blackfeet fled into a thicket of willows; when our people surrounded them, and kept up a heavy firing upon them from every side till night, but as is supposed not with much effect as they acknowledge only two or three being wounded. The part of the willows where they are, was occupied by a party of F[lat]heads last season, who similarly situated, made a number of huts to hide in. The Indians propose keeping a strict watch all night, and keeping them from escaping so that the attack may be renewed in the morning. Here we had an opportunity of seeing the Indian mode of fighting.

WEDNESDAY [January] 11. Very cold in the night and morning.

The Indians neglected their watch, and the Black-

243 Cumcarny, rather Cooncarny.

244 To Shoshone Cove. – J. E. R.

feet escaped towards morning. From the tracks three of them are supposed to be killed or badly wounded. On examining the place where they were it is a wonder some of them were not killed, the willows were completely lashed with the balls. It is to be regretted the Indians did not keep better watch as it would not have been difficult to have stormed the place, and killed the whole of them. They had some conversation with a woman of their own nation who is with us, and told her that the Americans have a fort at the falls of the Missouri;[245] that the Blackfeet have provided themselves with a great quantity of arms and ammunition, and are assembling in great force to come, and attack the F[lat]heads in the Spring.

Raised camp, and proceeded down the river two hours, six miles to below our camp at the fork.[246] Not a buffalo to be seen though great numbers were here yesterday but were raised by the firing yesterday.

THURSDAY [January] 12. Stormy, cold weather.

Raised camp, and proceeded up the main fork two and one-half hours, eight miles. Our object is to find buffalo.[247] Some bulls were seen, and the Indians report that some cows were seen ahead. We are encamped in a clump of poplar, but very indifferent feeding for the horses. The buffalo have eaten up what little grass [there] was, short way farther down the river there is good grass.

FRIDAY [January] 13. Blew a storm in the night and all day.

Did not raise camp. The unfavorable weather de-

245 Fort Piegan at mouth of Marias River. – J. E. R.

246 To mouth of Red Rock Creek, near Armstead. – P. C. P.

247 Up Red Rock Creek to near Redrock, Montana. – J. E. R.

terred the people from going after buffalo. Some bulls were killed.

SATURDAY [January] 14. Stormy and very cold.

Did not raise camp. Some Indians unknown to the chiefs raised the buffalo which are ahead, which will probably be the cause of our returning down the river again.

SUNDAY [January] 15. Still stormy, cold weather.

Raised camp and moved down the river to near the fork.[248] No buffalo to be seen, all hands, whites and Indians are short of food.

MONDAY [January] 16. Cloudy weather milder these days past.

Raised camp and proceeded down the river two and one-half hours, seven miles to near our encampment of the [26]. Not a buffalo to be seen, but the people were out hunting in the mountains, and both whites and Indians killed several sheep which is a most seasonable supply as several of the people are short of food.

TUESDAY [January] 17. Cloudy, cold weather.

Continued our route down the river, four and one-half hours, fifteen miles to near our encampment of the twentieth of November.[249] There are buffalo along the mountains on both sides of the river but at a considerable distance. Some were also seen a short way down the river not so far off.

WEDNESDAY [January] 18. Cloudy, cold weather.

Continued our route down the river two hours, six miles.[250] Immediately on encamping all hands went in pursuit of buffalo, and returned in the evening loaded

248 Fork of Red Rock and Horse Prairie Creeks. — P. C. P.

249 Near Dillon, Montana. — P. C. P.

250 Down to the Beaverhead below Dillon. — P. C. P.

with meat, which is very acceptable. Buffalo are very numerous here; they are pushing this way, and supposed to be driven by the Pd Oreilles or Blackfeet. Our people killed thirty-seven.

THURSDAY [January] 19. Mild weather.

Did not raise camp, the most of the people both Indians and whites were hunting buffalo, and killed a great number. Our people killed thirty-three. A young man arrived from Pd Oreille[251] camp in the evening; it is three short days' journey distant.

FRIDAY [January] 20. Raw, cold weather.

All hands again in pursuit of buffalo. Our people killed twenty-seven. In the evening L. Randeau and M. Plante arrived from the Pd Oreille camp,[252] and brought our letters from the Fort.[253]

SATURDAY [January] 21. Cloudy, cold weather.

But few of the people went in pursuit of buffalo as they were too far off. A party of five Americans arrived at our camp from Salmon River, the most of them afoot. The Blackfeet have stolen several of their horses.

SUNDAY [January] 22. Fine, mild weather.

This being Sunday we did not raise camp. Some lodges of Indians went ahead.

MONDAY [January] 23. Rained in the night, stormy cold weather.

Raised camp and marched three hours, ten miles N.

251 The Pend d'Oreille camp. Evidently in the Bitter Root valley.—P. C. P.

252 Randeau had been left sick at Walla Walla, September 9. M. Plante had deserted on October 24.—P. C. P.

253 Probably Flathead House the post on the north bank of Clark's Fork, Sanders County, Montana, near site of present Northern Pacific Railroad station of Eddy. David Thompson's original Salish House (1809) was some ten miles down river (S. W.) David Thompson, *Narrative*, 375, 418. Ross Cox, *Columbia River*, i, 231.—W. S. L.

N. W. to the little river[254] where we encamped on the [?]. The Indians who were encamped here are a little below us. Buffalo were very numerous here a few days ago; now they are all driven off to the mountains.

TUESDAY [January] 24. Very cold weather.

Did not raise camp. Some buffalo in the mountains but none near.

WEDNESDAY [January] 25. Cloudy weather, some snow during the day.

Did not raise camp. Last night the Blackfeet stole eleven horses from the Indians, six from the Americans who are with us, including four of old Charley's, a colt belonging to Toupe which was left out of the guard, and killed a poor mare which was also left out. They left a gun, a robe, etc., when they took the Indians' horses.

THURSDAY [January] 26. Fine weather.

The Blackfeet again visited us last night, and stole three horses, belonging to our people, all very lean, one of them fell in the river crossing, and was drowned. They also stole another horse from the Indians and one from the Americans.

FRIDAY [January] 27. Mild weather, light snow.

Did not raise camp, and some of the people killed a few buffalo. The Americans went off. These two days several lodges of Indians left us, and went to the Pd Oreille camp. Finished some letters to send below.

SATURDAY [January] 28. Cloudy, mild weather.

Raised camp and proceeded three hours, ten miles S. S. W. to a small fork near the mountains.[255] A herd of buffalo were driven down from the hills, and sev-

[254] Probably Birch Creek. – P. C. P.

[255] Probably up Birch Creek. – P. C. P.

eral of them killed by the people and the Indians. Several of the Indians left us, and went to join the Pd Oreille camp. Only twelve or fifteen lodges remain with us now.

SUNDAY [January] 29. Cloudy, rather cold weather.

Did not raise camp, on account of one of the women being brought to bed and another being sick. No buffalo to be seen near.

MONDAY [January] 30. Cloudy, mild, but rather cold weather.

At break of day this morning we were attacked by a party of at least three hundred Blackfeet, they continued the battle to noon when they retired, and were pursued by a party of our people but were too numerous to be attacked successfully, and after some sharp firing were allowed to retire [we retired]. They commenced the attack in the morning by a war yell and a discharge of guns, and were promptly met by part of our people and the Indians who returned the fire with effect which made them retire a little, and take positions in the woods and on the hills overlooking the camp. Some of them were wounded and several killed at the offset. Two of our men W. Raymond and Bt. Gadipre were wounded, one of our Indians was killed and two wounded. A brisk fire was kept up on both sides to noon, at one time they had surrounded our camp, but kept at a considerable distance. Our cannon burst the third discharge, one of the killed was scalped by our people, he is supposed to be a chief from the efforts they made to recover his body, four or five others were killed, and several wounded, but they succeeded in carrying them off. Our loss is a F[lat]head killed and three wounded, two whites, W. Raymond wounded dangerously, Bt. Gadipre severely but not dangerously, and my little W[alla] W[alla] I[n]d[ian] house-keeper dangerously wounded, S. Kanato slightly wounded in the foot, and myself slightly in the arm. The F[lat]heads have six and us five horses killed and several wounded. Nearly the whole of them were armed with guns, and well supplied with ammunition, as they were enabled to keep up a brisk and continued fire upon us for upwards of five hours. The old chief[256] had two horses killed under him. They were however repulsed.

TUESDAY [January] 31. Snowed most of the day.

Did not raise camp owing to our wounded people and the bad weather. The Blackfeet after leaving us yesterday, fell in with four lodges of F[lat]heads coming from the Pd Oreille camp to join us. They abandoned the baggage, and escaped with the horses, the Blackfeet [burnt] the property. They had some conversation at a distance, the party were chiefly Blood Indians and Big Bellies, the one who was killed at our camp was the chief, he wished the [Piegans][257] to accompany him on this expedition, but the chief refused and said he wished to come and make peace with the F[lat]heads in the summer, the other replied that he would go with his own party, and wholly destroy the whites and F[lat]heads, and that they would find only the bones to make peace with. He has been disappointed, and his own carcass remains on the ground.

WEDNESDAY [February] 1. Snowed the most of the day.

[256] The old Flathead chief, La Bunte.

[257] Bancroft MS. Piegans. – P. C. P.

Did not raise camp, owing to the F[lat]heads going for their friends who were pillaged by the B[lack]feet yesterday. Some of the B[lack]feet stole six of our people's horses last night which were allowed to pass the guard by the negligence of the men who were on watch. These two days some of the B[lack]feet's dogs have been taken with bundles of shoes, and other articles tied upon them,[258] there was some ammunition also.

THURSDAY [February] 2. Snowed part of the day.

Did not raise camp, waiting for the few F[lat]heads who have not yet come up. The W[alla] W[alla] Indian who was wounded died last night. He suffered dreadfully for a few hours previous to his decease. The poor fellow received the ball in the side, and it took a direction towards the backbone.

FRIDAY [February] 3. Cloudy, cold weather.

The Indians for whom we were waiting arrived in the night. Raised camp and proceeded down the little river two hours, six miles S. E., and encamped at a good feeding place for the horses.[259] It was our intention to cut across the mountains to Cumcarny, which is the shortest road, but there is too much snow, and we took our old road. Our wounded people suffer much in removal, such a misfortune situated as we are renders us wretched indeed.

SATURDAY [February] 4. Very cold in the night, some light snow during the day.

Did not raise camp. Some of the people went after buffalo, and killed two. The Indians also killed a few.

SUNDAY [February] 5. Snowed part of the day.

Did not raise camp. Our horses are feeding pretty

[258] Dogs were frequently made beasts of burden by the Indians.

[259] Down Birch Creek. – P. C. P.

well here, they are in much need of it, as from the severe cold weather for some time back they are falling off very much.

MONDAY [February] 6. Snowed in the morning, fine weather afterwards.

Moved camp, and marched two and one-half hours, seven miles S. E. to the main river a little above our camp of the twenty-fourth November.[260] Some herds of buffalo were seen along the mountains, the Indians and some of the people went in pursuit of them but with little success, as it was too late in the day.

TUESDAY [February] 7. Some snow in the morning, fine weather afterwards.

Did not raise camp. Four Indians started in the night to bring a large herd of buffalo from the mountains down to the level ground, and brought them part of the way, but the people from the camp advanced too soon, and they returned to the mountain, very few were killed, indeed the horses both the Ind[ians] and ours are living so bare that few of them can catch the buffalo. Our people killed a cow and two bulls.

WEDNESDAY [February] 8. Very cold in the night, and severe squall of wind and snow past noon.

Raised camp and proceeded up the river to above an encampment of the [26 November?]. Not a buffalo to be seen today, tho' there were several herds yesterday along the mountains.

THURSDAY [February] 9. Stormy but not cold weather, snowed a good deal in the night.

Continued our route up the river to near the fork.[261] Here we expected to find buffalo, but saw none.

---

260 To Beaverhead River near Dillon, Montana. – P. C. P.

261 Red Rock and Horse Prairie Creeks. – P. C. P.

FRIDAY [February] 10. Overcast weather, snow thawing a little.

Did not raise camp in order to allow a little repose to a wounded man. Our horses are also in much need of feeding and resting a little. Some of them gave up on the road yesterday. Some of the Indians were up the river on discovery, and report that there are a good many buffalo, but they are a good way off.

SATURDAY [February] 11. Stormy, raw weather.

Raised camp, and proceeded two hours, seven miles up the river[262] to near our encampment of the [Jan. 10]. All hands out in pursuit of buffalo. Our people killed nine. Several of the horses were not able to come with them, and several came home lame, it was bad ground where they ran them. The buffalo were on their way descending the river. Had we remained a day longer below, it would have been of advantage as the buffalo would have passed, and gone on ahead our road they are now driven back up the river.

SUNDAY [February] 12. Very cold in the night, and cold stormy weather with some snow during the day.

Did not raise camp. Here we have good feeding for the horses but fuel is scarce.

MONDAY [February] 13. Bitter cold weather in the night, and during the day.

Did not raise camp.

TUESDAY [February] 14. Very cold weather, did not raise camp. This intense cold weather is very hard upon our horses.

WEDNESDAY [February] 15. Bitter cold weather in the night and all day.

Did not raise camp. The poor horses ran in among

---

262 By Horse Prairie Creek to Shoshone Cove. – J. E. R.

the bushes, and would not venture out even to feed. One was dead in the morning, and two died during the day.

THURSDAY [February] 16. Weather milder than these days past.

Did not raise camp. Our poor horses fed little today.

FRIDAY [February] 17. Some snow and blowing in the morning, fine weather afterwards.

Did not raise camp. Our horses fed well today. Some of the people went in quest of buffalo, and killed three. There are considerable numbers in the hills hard bye, but the snow in the ravines is very deep, and difficult to cross with horses.

SATURDAY [February] 18. Thick fog in the morning, fine weather afterwards.

Did not raise camp. It was arraigned in the morning with the Indians that all hands were to go and surround the buffalo, but the greater part of the Indians afterwards raised camp, and went on a piece ahead. Several of the people went in quest of buffalo but with little success.

SUNDAY [February] 19. Foggy in the morning, clear, cold weather afterwards.

Raised camp and proceeded on to where the Indians are encamped where we stopped, as had we gone farther we might have raised the buffalo, and it would have been too late to run them.

MONDAY [February] 20. Very cold in the night and all day.

The cold deterred us from raising camp. The poor horses are freezing.

TUESDAY [February] 21. Snowing, blowing, drifting, and very cold all day.

Did not raise camp, we are like to freeze with cold.

WEDNESDAY [February] 22. Clear, very cold weather.

Raised camp and proceeded up the river to a little above our encampment of 1 December.[263] There are plenty of buffalo above too but it is too late to go in quest of them today. Good feeding for the horses but wood is scarce.

THURSDAY [February] 23. A most freezing, bitter cold night, the weather became overcast, and was pretty mild during the day.

All hands whites and Indians went in pursuit of buffalo, and killed several. The horses are so lean and feeble that few of them can easily catch a buffalo. Our people killed seven.

FRIDAY [February] 24. Cloudy, rather mild weather.

Did not raise camp. No buffalo are to be seen now. Some of the young men went to drive an immense number of them that are not far off this way.

SATURDAY [February] 25. Cold, raw weather.

The most of the young men who went to bring the buffalo returned, without going the length of them.

SUNDAY [February] 26. Weather milder than these days past.

Large herds of buffalo were seen coming over the hills towards our camp towards evening but the noise at the camp over the river turned them back. A. Finlay arrived in the evening, he stopped out last night, and killed three buffalo.

MONDAY [February] 27. Fine weather, the snow thawed a good deal on the low ground.

263 Bancroft MS. reads "10."

Several of the men and Indians went after buffalo. The most of our people returned late at night. They killed four buffalo. The Indians, slept out, to push the buffalo this way.

TUESDAY [February] 28. Fine mild weather, the snow on the low ground wasting fast.

A herd of buffalo was observed close to the camp early in the morning, and all hands went in pursuit of them by sunrise, our people killed six, and the Indians several, a number of horses were not able to come up with them. Some of our people who slept out last night returned; they killed six buffalo–the Indians also returned.

WEDNESDAY [February] 29. Some light snow in the morning. Fine mild weather the snow thawing afterwards. Some of the people went in quest of buffalo but with little success.

THURSDAY [March] 1. Blowing pretty fresh, the snow thawing.

Raised camp and made up the river to near an encampment of the [?]. Large herds of buffalo were feeding not far from the camp, all hands went in pursuit of them, and killed several. Our people killed twelve.

FRIDAY [March] 2. Fine weather, snow thawing.

Did not raise camp. Some of the people went in pursuit of buffalo, and killed five.

SATURDAY [March] 3. Weather as yesterday.

Did not raise camp. Five young men left for Salmon River. Some of our people went in pursuit of buffalo, and killed three.

SUNDAY [March] 4. Overcast fine weather, snow thawing.

Did not raise camp. No buffalo to be seen near. The young men who started for Salmon River yesterday returned, they say there is too much snow in the mountains.

MONDAY [March] 5. Mild weather.

Raised camp and moved up the river to near our encampment of [?]. The snow melting a good deal. Some of the buffalo were seen. Some of the people went after them, but there was too much snow, and they could not come up with them.

TUESDAY [March] 6. Fine weather, snow thawing fast in the low ground.

A herd of buffalo were observed descending the mountains. Several of the people went in pursuit of them, but the snow was so deep that very few of them could be killed; people killed only three bulls.

WEDNESDAY [March] 7. Fine weather.

Raised camp and proceeded up the river[264] to near our encampment of [Jan. 27]. There still appears a good deal of snow on the mountain but there are three or four roads of buffalo, so that we expect to find a track round.

THURSDAY [March] 8. Cloudy, raw weather, the snow thawed fast in the middle of the day.

Did not raise camp in order to let our weak horses rest before taking the mountain. Numbers of them are very weak, and are giving up short as the encampment was.

FRIDAY [March] 9. Stormy but thawing part of the day.

Raised camp and crossed the height of land[265] to

[264] Up Horse Prairie Creek.—P. C. P.

[265] Bannack Pass. Usually mispelled Bannock.—J. E. R.

near our encampment of 4 Jan[uar]y. Found a good deal of snow at the north side of the hill; it was very hard and fatiguing on the first horses. Afterwards we found a well beaten buffalo road. The horses were much fatigued, and some of them with difficulty reached the encampment. This was a hard day on our poor wounded man.

SATURDAY [March] 10. A violent storm of snow in the forepart of the night; fine weather during the day.

Raised camp and proceeded to Salmon River a little above the poplar fork.[266] Here there is good feeding for the horses, and no snow except what fell last night. Some herds of buffalo were observed towards the height of land, and all hands went in pursuit of them, several of the horses were not able to catch them as they fled into the snow which is very hard. Our people killed only five. The Indians saw some marks of Blackfeet in the mountains yesterday.

SUNDAY [March] 11. Snowed all night, about nine inches deep of snow fell, raw cold weather during the day. Some of the people went after buffalo today.

MONDAY [March] 12. Fine weather, snow thawed a little in the middle of the day.

The people were again in quest of buffalo but with little success, the most of the horses are now too weak. Our men killed four.

TUESDAY [March] 13. Raw weather in the morning, snow thawed a little in the middle of the day.

All hands were in pursuit of buffalo, but scarcely a

266 Fork: Texas and Timber Creek, which last is studded with cottonwood trees belonging to the *populus genus.* – J. E. R.

horse either of ours or the Indians could come up with them. Our people killed only two.

WEDNESDAY [March] 14. Raw, cold weather, snow thawed very little.

Many of the people were in quest of buffalo today, only one herd was seen in the mountains. It is supposed they are driven across the height of land. Three Indians arrived from the N[ez] P[ercé] camp at the fork of the river.[267] The Americans are off some time ago. No buffalo below. William Raymond, our unfortunate man who was wounded on the 30 Jan[uar]y, died this afternoon. He was reduced to a mere skeleton; he had taken scarcely any nourishment since he was wounded. The wound was mortified.

THURSDAY [March] 15. Cold weather, thawing a little in the middle of the day.

Did not raise camp. A herd of buffalo passed in the evening, one of them was killed. Some others were seen coming from the mountains. It is supposed they were disturbed by Blackfeet.

FRIDAY [March] 16. Cloudy, thawing.

Raised camp and proceeded a few miles down the river to below poplar fork, and encamped at a good feeding place for the horses.

SATURDAY [March] 17. Cloudy, soft weather.

Did not raise camp. Last night a party of Blackfeet horse thieves had the audacity to come into the camp, notwithstanding the moon was so clear that it was nearly as clear as day, and stole four of the Indians' horses that were tied at the lodges, two from each end of the camp, they also took the poor horse belonging to our

[267] At Salmon City.—J. E. R.

people that had been turned out of the guard to feed. One belonging to R. Cook [one] to P. B[irnie], and one L. Riendeau. Two young men of the Indians pursued them, and came up with them that were behind the rest, whom they attacked and killed after a sharp battle, and brought the scalps to the camp about nine o'clock in the morning. One of them was wounded in the arm by an arrow. They have found our people's miserable horses, but they were so knocked up that they could not bring them on, moreover they heard the war cry of some more of the Blackfeet in the hills, and did not deem it prudent to delay. They consider the party of Blackfeet altogether to consist of fifty to sixty men; they had two lodges in the defile.

SUNDAY [March] 18. Fair weather in the morning, but became stormy with snow and sleet afterwards.

Raised camp and proceeded ten miles down the river,[268] and encamped at a fine feeding place for the horses. It was very unpleasant marching, but the bad weather did not set in till we were getting under way.

MONDAY [March] 19. Fair weather.

Did not raise camp in order to allow the horses to feed. All the Indians but two lodges went on ahead. Three Indians arrived from the Pd. Oreille.

TUESDAY [March] 20. Fine weather.

Continued our route ten miles down the river to below the lower defile to Cumcarny.[269] No buffalo to be seen, a large herd of elk were observed on the mountains. Some of the people went in pursuit of them but without success.

WEDNESDAY [March] 21. Fine weather.

---

268 Lemhi Pass. – J. E. R.

269 Agency Creek. Defile of Cum Carney = Lemhi Pass. – P. C. P.

Continued our journey down the river to a little above the grand camp of the N[ez] P[ercé] F[lat]-head Indians.[270] In the afternoon after encamping, a youth M. Plante's brother-in-law aged sixteen or seventeen years, ate hemlock root in a mistake; was poisoned, and died in a short time. When he was found he was too far gone for any remedy to be applied. A child of J. S. Loranger's, six weeks old[271] who has been sick for some time, also died.

THURSDAY [March] 22. Fine weather.

Moved a few miles down the river to near the Indian camp, and in a short time were visited by most of the Indians. Our object in coming was to obtain information relative to the route we mean to pursue.

FRIDAY [March] 23. Cold, stormy weather, some light snow showers.

Did not raise camp [sic]. Did not raise camp.

SATURDAY [March] 24. Raw, cold weather.

Raised camp and cut across the [part?] nine miles to the principal fork near the rocks,[272] and encamped at a good feeding place for the horses. Several of the Indians accompanied us. We are glad to get away from them for the Nez Percés are really an annoyance.

SUNDAY [March] 25. Did not raise camp. Four men are preparing to descend the river in a canoe to hunt this evening to the fort,[273] it is expected they will make a good hunt. Several more Indians visited us.

[270] A joint winter camp of the Nez Percé and Flathead Indians at the Lewis and Clark fish weirs on Lemhi River. – J. E. R.

[271] Six weeks old, born during the expedition; pregnant Indian and half-breed women often accompanied their husbands on such expeditions. – W. S. L.

[272] Salmon River at commencement of the gorge six miles south of Salmon City. – J. E. R.

[273] Fort Walla Walla. – P. C. P.

MONDAY [March] 26. Fine weather.

Raised camp and proceeded eight miles up the river.[274] Four men, L. Boisdnt, A. Dumaris, M. Plante, and J. Laurin left in a small skin canoe to descend the river, and hunt their way down. It is expected they will make a good hunt as this part of the river is not known to have ever been hunted by whites. Lewis and Clark passed down this in canoes.[275]

TUESDAY [March] 27. Showery weather.

Proceeded up the river ten miles.[276] Some N[ez] P[ercé] Ind[ians] joined us yesterday evening.

WEDNESDAY [March] 28. Heavy rain the most of the day.

Proceeded seven miles up the river. There are plenty of sheep on the mountains. The river is rising fast these two days.

THURSDAY [March] 29. Showery weather.

Continued our journey ten miles up the river. The road very hilly and fatiguing for the horses. Great numbers of sheep on the hills. The people killed several of them.

FRIDAY [March] 30. Raw, cold weather.

Did not raise camp in order to allow the horses to repose and feed.

SATURDAY [March] 31. Raw, cold weather.

Raised camp and moved up the river eight miles to

---

274 Up Salmon River. – P. C. P.

275 In August, 1805, the Lewis and Clark party traversed much the same ground as Work from the forks west of Gallatin up the Jefferson to what they termed "Shoshone Cove" and across the divide by "Lewis and Clark pass" – Lemhi Pass – to the Salmon; thence across to the Bitter Root and down to the vicinity of Missoula and Lolo Pass. See *Original Lewis & Clark Journals*, Thwaites ed., vol. 2, and *Atlas*, map 30, plates i, ii, and iii. – W. S. L.

276 Up Salmon River to near Poison Creek. – J. E. R.

Bluffs along the Salmon River

This locality was the famous camping ground for the Blackfoot, Flathead, Nez Percés, and Shoshone Indians during the early part of the nineteenth century and a gathering place for Indians even at the present time.

McKay's defile.[277] Plenty of sheep on the hills. No buffalo to be seen.

SUNDAY [April] 1. Cold weather, a heavy hail shower in the afternoon. Did not raise camp.

MONDAY [April] 2. Fine weather, but cold.

Did not raise camp. The people out in different directions hunting, some sheep were killed. Some buffalo were seen, but none killed.

TUESDAY [April] 3. Fine weather.

Moved up the river seven miles. Here we have good feeding for the horses; the hills close to the river and low ground have been clear of snow for a length of time, and vegetation is considerable advanced; the young grass is a good length. The hills a little farther from the river are still covered with snow, and along the shores of the river the ice remains a considerable thickness. Several of the people out with their traps. But little signs of beaver.

WEDNESDAY [April] 4. Fine weather.

Did not raise camp. Two men A. Finlay, J. Favel were off since yesterday morning examining a small river where it was expected some beaver would be found, but there are none. Some more of the men were off visiting some of the small forks but without success. A. Longtin took one beaver.

THURSDAY [April] 5. Fine, warm weather.

Moved up the river ten miles, and encamped at the

---

[277] So named from Charles McKay, a son, by an Indian mother, of Alexander McKay of the Astor party who met a tragic end on the destruction of the Tonquin. Charles McKay had accompanied Mr. Ogden to this neighborhood in 1825-6. Washington Historical Society *Quarterly*, v. 189-191.—W. S. L.

Mr. Rees differs on this point and explains it as follows: So called because Thomas McKay wintered on this stream in 1827. Now called the Pahsimaroi.—P. C. P.

hot spring.[278] The men visited several traps which they had set, but found nothing. All hands went in pursuit of buffalo, and killed eight; they are very lean.

FRIDAY [April] 6. Fine weather, but cold in the night and mornings – the snow still lies deep in the mountains, and it is not long since it went off the low ground; there are large banks of ice along the shores of the river. Here we intended to take into the mountains to the plain where we expected to find some beaver, but cannot on account of the snow so that we must go around.

Did not raise camp, in order to allow the horses to feed, tho the grass is but indifferent.

SATURDAY [April] 7. Fine weather.

Continued our route fifteen miles up a little fork, and encamped at what is called the fountain.[279] The people went after buffalo, and killed nine; they are mostly very lean.

SUNDAY [April] 8. Fine weather.

Did not raise camp in order to allow the horses to rest, and feed a little after the long day's march they made yesterday. The grass here is very indifferent as the snow has but shortly gone off the ground, and the swamp is still frozen. There appears a good deal of snow in the height of land ahead of us. The people went in pursuit of buffalo, and killed four.

MONDAY [April] 9. Rather cold weather.

Proceeded across the height of land to the fountain in Goddin's defile.[280] There is a good deal of snow on

278 East side of Salmon River near Challis. – J. E. R.

279 Swamp, called Thousand Springs. See Oregon Historical Society *Quarterly*, xiii, 369. – W. S. L.

280 Big Lost River in Thousand Spring valley. – J. E. R. The Goodin's River of Alexander Ross, *Fur Hunters*, ii, 124-5. Discovered by Thyery

the height of land, and the snow has not been long off the ground here; a few buffalo were to be seen at a distance.

TUESDAY [April] 10. Raw, cold weather.

Did not raise camp in order to allow the horses to feed and repose. The grass is but indifferent.

WEDNESDAY [April] 11. Snowed in the night and forepart of the day.

The unfavorable weather deterred us from raising camp. It was our intention to have struck across the mountains to the head of Sukly [Sickly] [281] River but there is too much snow on the mountains so that we will be obliged to go by other road.

THURSDAY [April] 12. Rather cold, but fine weather.

(Henry) Godin in 1820, whose name appears as numbers 843, 677, and 576 respectively on the lists of employees of the Hudson's Bay Company in North America for the years 1821-1824, one of the many Iroquois Indians introduced into the Rocky Mountain district by the Northwesterners and Hudson's Bay Company traders. J. B. Godin of the line appears in the Northwest Company list of 1804 as a voyageur at Rivere du Sauteux, Masson, *Des Bourgeois*, i, 411. Thyery Godin was with Alexander Ross' Snake River expedition in 1824. He afterwards deserted on May 24, 1825, with the Canadians and entered the employ of Sublette, and was later murdered on the river which took his name, which he had discovered in 1820. Washington Historical Society *Quarterly*, xiv, 381. Godin's River rises in Custer County, Idaho, and, breaking through the mountains to the south opposite the east branch of the Malades (or Little Wood River), by a defile or canyon called "Godin's defile," turns to the northeast and in forty miles is lost by sinking in the lava flows of eastern Idaho. The river is now known as the Big Lost River. In Washington Irving's *Captain Bonneville*, chapters xv and xvi, mention is made of the Godin's River and defile, and in chapter vi, of Antoine Godin, his son, mentioned as an employee of Sublette near Pierre's Hole. For further reference to Godin see: Victor, *River of the West* (1870), 129-130; Townsend's *Narrative* (1839), 114.—W. S. L.

[281] Sickly River:—Probably over Ryan Pass to North Fork. Sickly River, now known as the Malade or Big Wood River; named the River aux Malades by Alexander Ross in 1824 on account of thirty-seven of his party being there made violently ill from eating "white" beaver, unfit for food

Raised camp and proceeded down the river [282] [?] miles. There were some buffalo here but they have fled down the river. Some of the people set a few traps.

FRIDAY [April] 13. Fine weather.

Continued our route down the river [ ] miles. Some of the people who went ahead raised the buffalo here, and they have fled farther down the river. Pichette took two beaver. The people killed three bulls.

SATURDAY [April] 14. Fine weather.

Continued our journey down the river nine miles. The most of the people set their traps. There are some signs of beaver. The buffalo are still ahead.

SUNDAY [April] 15. Fine weather.

Did not raise camp. Fifteen beaver and one otter were taken. There are plenty of buffalo a short way ahead. The people set some more traps.

MONDAY [April] 16. Fine weather.

Did not raise camp. Twelve beaver were taken; the people set some more traps.

TUESDAY [April] 17. Fine weather.

Moved camp a few miles down the river to find better feeding for the horses. The people moved down the river with the traps. Fifteen beaver were taken. Some of the people who went farther down the river saw some tracks of Blackfeet not very old.

WEDNESDAY [April] 18. Rained in the night, fine weather during the day.

Raised camp and moved three and one-half hours, eleven miles down the river. We had intended to strike across the mountains from our last station but

---

from feeding on poisonous plants. See Ross, *Fur Hunters of the Far West*, ii, 82-3, 115. – W. S. L.

282 Down Lost River. – H. F. H.

there is too much snow, and it would be too long to wait till it be practicable. The people out with their traps; six beaver taken. The people raised a large herd of buffalo, and killed fourteen of them.

THURSDAY [April] 19. Fine warm weather.

Did not raise camp in order to allow the people time to dry the meat that was killed yesterday, and to let the horses feed. The people out with their traps; one beaver taken. Set fire to the plain, and the smoke will probably drive off all the buffalo.

FRIDAY [April] 20. Fine weather.

Moved down the river three hours, ten miles E. No buffalo to be seen, the fire yesterday has driven them all off. The people out with their traps, but little or no appearance of beaver. Some tracks of Blackfeet not very old to be seen.

SATURDAY [April] 21. Fine weather.

Marched three and three-fourths hours, twelve miles S. S. E., and encamped at a fine feeding place for the horses. Five men went ahead to hunt a little fork.[283]

SUNDAY [April] 22. Fine weather.

Did not raise camp.

MONDAY [April] 23. Stormy weather in the afternoon.

Raised camp and proceeded three and one-half hours, twelve miles S. S. E. Road rocky. We intended to strike across the mountains[284] at our last station, but there appeared too much snow, and we have to go round. Some Blackfoot Indians were prowling about our camp last night. A short way from the camp this morning the tracks of twenty-five or thirty men were

[283] Mouth of Antelope Creek. – J. E. R.

[284] Lost River Mountains. – H. F. H.

seen. They struck down into the rocks. Five Blackfeet were descried immediately afterwards, and pursued but the ground was so stony that they could not be overtaken. They threw away their clothes in their haste. They are a war party returning from the Snakes.

TUESDAY [April] 24. Stormy weather, heavy showers of rain.

Continued our route four and one-half hours, sixteen miles S. S. E. along the foot of the mountains[285] to river a *Bastin*.[286] The road in places stony. The men who left on the 21 returned with twenty beaver. Two of them, Gadipré and Rodin, were kept in a hill part of the day yesterday and all night by some Blackfeet. A Blackfoot descended from the hills in the evening, and attempted to steal a horse but was discovered, unfortunately the horse keeper had not his gun with him or he might have killed him.

WEDNESDAY [April] 25. Overcast, very heavy rain in the greater part of the day.

Raised camp and proceeded three hours, nine miles S. to a little river. All hands proceeded up the river with the traps. There are some signs of beaver but the water is very high so that it is difficult to discover where they are.

THURSDAY [April] 26. Very heavy rain in the night, some light showers during the day.

Did not raise camp. The people visited their traps, and set more. Five beaver were taken.

FRIDAY [April] 27. Cloudy, stormy weather.

Did not raise camp. The people went to visit their

285 Along the foot of the Lost River Mountains. – P. C. P.

286 Stream made by high water. – J. E. R.

traps, but one of the men, Toupe, saw the children of the camp playing, and mistook them for Blackfeet, and went off full speed after their men, and stated that the camp was attacked, and all our horses taken. This made the people return before they had visited their traps. Twenty-nine beaver were taken.

SATURDAY [April] 28. Stormy, cloudy weather.

Did not raise camp. The people visited their traps, and reset several of them. Fourteen beaver were taken. The people not having put the traps in order yesterday was the cause of so few beaver being taken.

SUNDAY [April] 29. Cloudy, stormy weather, some light showers.

Did not raise camp. Twenty-six beaver taken. The men took up their traps, they thought they were too far off. Had they left them down another night they would have caught some more beaver. A band of buffalo were seen on the hills in the evening they were marching fast, and were probably raised by Blackfoot Indians.

MONDAY [April] 30. Cloudy, showery weather, blowing fresh.

Raised camp and proceeded three hours, ten miles S. S. W. to the Grand Masky.[287] Several of the men proceeded ahead, and set the traps in Sulky [Sickly] River; others examined the Masky, but saw so little signs of beaver that they did not set the traps.

TUESDAY [May] 1. Stormy weather, hail and rain showers in the morning.

Raised camp and proceeded three hours, ten miles S. S. W. to Sulky [Sickly] River.[288] The most of the

[287] South branch Antelope Creek. – J. E. R.

[288] East Fork Little Wood River. – H. F. H.

men proceeded, some up and some down the river, and set their traps. The appearance of a good many beaver. The traps set yesterday only produced eleven. The river has been lately very high, but the water has fallen considerably.

WEDNESDAY [May] 2. Stormy weather, showers of hail and rain.

Did not raise camp. The people out with their traps. Thirty-six beaver taken.

THURSDAY [May] 3. Stormy, showery weather.

Did not raise camp. The people visiting their traps, and setting more. Twenty-five beaver taken. L. Quintalle saw four Blackfeet ascending a hill attempting to approach him as he was setting his traps in a small fork. They are supposed to be part of a gang that are lurking in the mountains, seeking an opportunity to kill and steal. The tracks of some Snakes[289] are seen about the river near our camp, but none of them venture near us.

FRIDAY [May] 4. Still stormy, showery weather.

Did not raise camp. The people out at their traps. Twenty-four beaver and two otter taken. No tracks of the enemy to be seen, the men keep a good lookout as they are afraid of being murdered while visiting their traps. The river is thickly wooded, thicketty and difficult to approach. F. Payette killed two bulls.

SATURDAY [May] 5. Stormy and violent shower of rain and hail.

The people visited and reset their traps. Nineteen beaver and one otter taken. No tracks of the enemy to be seen. The men are becoming less afraid. It is supposed the party in the mountains are but a few in

[289] Shoshone Indians. – J. E. R.

number probably remaining with some sick or wounded companions.

SUNDAY [May] 6. Heavy rain and hail in the night, stormy, showery during the day.

Did not raise camp. The people are out at their traps. Thirty beaver taken. No tracks of Blackfeet to be seen.

MONDAY [May] 7. Stormy, cold weather.

Moved two miles up the river[290] in order to find better feeding for the horses. The men visited their traps. Seventeen beaver and one otter taken.

TUESDAY [May] 8. Heavy rain the greater part of the day.

I intended to raise camp and proceed up the river but was deterred by the bad weather. The men out at their traps. Twelve beaver taken. A party of Nez Percés, nine men and two women with thirty to forty horses, arrived in the evening from their own lands on their way to join some of their people at Salmon River. Two of our men, G. Plante and C. Riendeau, were coming from their traps, and saw these people who they mistook for a party of Blackfeet, and were so frightened that they did not attend to the calls and friendly signals of the Indians but fled full speed to the camp, and related that the Blackfeet had killed all our people who were up the river with their traps, and had pursued themselves for their lives. All hands were now busily employed tying the horses when the Indians arrived and undeceived us.

WEDNESDAY [May] 9. Cold, showery weather.

Did not raise camp. Owing to the quantity of snow

[290] Little Wood River. Work's plans apparently were to go to the sources of the Wood River, then across to the east fork of the Salmon. — P. C. P.

which still appears on the mountains, it is apprehended we would not be able to pass, and if we could pass that the small creeks could not yet be hunted; we have therefore deferred crossing the mountains for the present, but intend to proceed a little to the southward where we will find good feeding for our horses, and expect to get a few beaver. Perhaps we may find another road by Read's River to cross the mountains. The head of Read's River [291] is not known to have ever been trapped by whites, and is said to be rich in beaver. The people visited their traps. Forty beaver and one otter taken. The most of the people up the river took up their traps.

THURSDAY [May] 10. Cloudy, cold weather.

[291] Read's River: – South fork of the Boise. This was a very good beaver stream. It was so named after John Read, a clerk in the Pacific (Astor) Fur Company, who came overland in 1811, and who accompanied Alexander MacKenzie on his Snake River expedition of 1812-3. After the failure of the Astor enterprise he was sent out from Astoria to the mountain passes in the Snake River country in the fall of 1813. Here his entire party was murdered and their goods plundered by the Ban-at-tee Indians in the late fall of 1813. Ban-at-tee was meant for the Bannocks. They were really mountain Snakes, or Tuknoika, or Sheep Eaters. See Ross Cox, *Columbia River*, i, 252-7; Franchere's *Narrative* (1820) 214-16; Ross, *Oregon Settlers*, 276-280; Irving, *Astoria* (1836) ii, 254-6. These Ban-at-tee Indians were a branch of the Snake Indians, known as the "Robber of Mountain" Snakes. See Ross, *Fur Hunters*, i, 249-250, 257. At p. 278, *Oregon Settlers*, Ross dubs them the "Dog-rib" tribe. The stream is referred to by Ross as Reid's River, *ibid.*, 91, 98. It is now known as the Boise River. Both MacKenzie and Read had built houses in the vicinity in 1812-3, Ross, *Oregon Settlers*, 278.

Boise River is called Roussie River in Minutes of Council of 1835. The name Boise is variously spelled in early journals and the Hudson's Bay Company fort at the mouth of the river appears as Fort Boisse, Fort Boissi, and Fort Borssie in the Minutes of Council for 1839, 1840, and 1843. It is said that the stream was given its present name by members of Captain Bonneville's expedition from the exclamations of the Canadian-French members – "*Les bois, les bois! Voyes les bois!*" – on account of the luxuriant growth of poplars along the stream – a welcome sight to the men who had struggled through dusty miles of sage brush country. – W. S. L.

Did not raise camp; waiting for four men who had their traps too far off to bring yesterday. Six beaver taken. There are a good many buffalo up the river.

FRIDAY [May] 11. Cloudy, cold weather.

Raised camp and proceeded two and one-half hours, eight miles S. S. W. across a point to a small creek.[292] Some of the people ahead with their traps. Four beaver taken.

SATURDAY [May] 12. Continued our route three hours, ten miles S. S. W. to another small creek.[293] The people visited the traps and setting more. Ten beaver taken. There are a few beaver, but they are shy, and difficult to take. The hunters who were ahead of the camp started eight buffalo which they pursued, but were only able to kill an old bull. In the evening some bulls were observed descending from the mountains, they were immediately pursued and three of them were killed. They were very lean which is rather surprising as there has been fine grass about this plain [place?] for a length of time.

SUNDAY [May] 13. Fine, warm weather.

Did not raise camp. The people visited their traps and set more. Eighteen beaver and [ ] otter taken.

MONDAY [May] 14. Fine, warm weather.

Did not raise camp. The people visited their traps. Seventeen beaver taken.

TUESDAY [May] 15. Fine, warm weather.

Raised camp and proceeded three and one-half hours, twelve miles. The peorle visited their traps. Twenty-nine beaver and three otters taken. The most of the people who were behind took up their traps.

---

292 Near Bellevue on Big Wood River. – J. E. R.

293 Camas Creek. – J. E. R.

WEDNESDAY [May] 16. Stormy weather.

Did not raise camp. The people visited their traps, and several were out setting more. Twelve beaver taken. Some of the people went ahead.

THURSDAY [May] 17. Fine weather.

Did not raise camp. The people took up their traps, as we mean to raise camp and proceed across the mountains to Read's River tomorrow. Eleven beaver and one otter taken, some elk and a black tail deer were killed.

FRIDAY [May] 18. Fine weather.

Raised camp and proceeded four hours, fourteen miles N.N.W. across the mountains, and encamped on a small fork which falls into Read's River.[294] The road for a mountain pretty good, but in places there were banks of snow and thick woods which were difficult to pass. From the height of land, the mountains towards the head of Read's River appear still deeply covered with snow, and the country altogether appears very mountainous. All hands out with the traps. Three beaver taken.

SATURDAY [May] 19. Fine weather, cold in the night.

Continued our route two hours, seven miles W.N.W. to one of the principal forks of Read's River which here runs from NN.E.[295] We crossed another fork of a smaller size which falls in from the N.E.[296] There is another large fork farther down which falls in from the N.W.[297] Part of the way today the road was very bad, very stony lying through thick woods. The coun-

[294] Up Willow Creek, across the mountains to Trail Creek. – J. E. R.

[295] Little Smoky. Should be S. S. E. – J. E. R.

[296] Big Smoky. – J. E. R.

[297] South fork Boise River. – J. E. R.

try is very mountainous, in places thickly wooded, and in places destitute of timber. All hands visited the traps. Thirty-six beaver taken besides nineteen brought by seven men who have been absent a few nights down the river. The people complain that beaver are very scarce, for a new country which this may be considered to be. The trappers under Mr. Ross[298] [were here] eight years ago but descended the river immediately, and did not stop to set traps, no other whites are known to have ever passed this way. The Indians frequently represent the head of this river as being very rich in beaver. Our object is to get to them, but from the appearance of the country we will probably have much difficulty. The Indians from whom some information might be obtained are so much afraid that they cannot be prevailed on to approach the camp. One of the men found four of them in the rocks yesterday, but they would not come to the camp. There were some others seen, but they fled on approach of the people. The men are directed to use every means to dispell their apprehensions.

SUNDAY [May] 20. Thunder, showery weather.

The water in the river rising. Did not raise camp. Some of the people towards the mountains are desiring to find a road to pass. F. Payette found five Snake Indians in the mountains, two of whom he prevailed upon to accompany him to the camp. From these we

298 Alexander Ross, a clerk of the original Pacific (Astor) Fur Company who entered the employ of the Northwest and Hudson's Bay Companies, and the author of *Adventures of the First Settlers on the Columbia River*, and *Fur Hunters of the Far West*, both dealing with the early fur trading enterprises in the Columbia River basin. His trading venture into the Snake River country and western Montana in 1824 is related in volume ii of the latter book on pp. 87. See also Oregon Historical Society *Quarterly*, xiv, no. 4. – W. S. L.

learned that the only pass in the mountains is by the fork to the westward. That on the other side of the mountain there is an extensive track of plain country well-stocked with beaver. The fork on which we are encamped takes its waters in the mountains not far from here, where it is formed by sundry branches. Nine beaver taken.

MONDAY [May] 21. Cloudy, fair weather.

Did not raise camp, in order to allow the people time to take up their traps. Nine beaver taken. The two Snakes who were brought to the camp yesterday were kindly treated, and received little presents, with which they were much pleased. They returned today accompanied by two more men and three women. These also received little presents. The account they give of the road and beaver accords with that given yesterday.

They promise to accompany us, and point out the passes in the mountains. We had an alarm of Blackfeet but it turns out to be nothing.

TUESDAY [May] 22. Cloudy, fine weather.

Raised camp and marched one and one-half hours, five miles W. across a point of hills to the western fork[299] where we encamped to await the Indians who promised to join us here.

WEDNESDAY [May] 23. Stormy, rather cold weather.

Did not raise camp. The Indians not coming to join us as they promised I took two of the young men, and went to find them, but they had fled. On returning from where they had been encamped one of the young men took another road, and found two of them but could not prevail upon them to accompany him, and

299 South fork of Boise near junction of Big Smoky. – J. E. R.

he did not like to use force. I ascended a high peak of the mountain to the northward to ascertain the appearance of the country behind. All in that direction appears a continuation of rugged mountains covered with snow.[300] A little to the westward the country appears lower, and not covered with snow. There appear two springs in the mountain, at the head of the river. Two men, Kanota and C. Plante, ascended a high peak to the westward, the country behind appeared pretty bare but still a considerable depth of snow on it. Some of the men went up towards the head of the river[301] with their traps; they found some beaver lodges but they are still frozen up. In this fork and the one behind the current is so strong and the banks and bed of the river so stony and gravelly that the beaver are unable to make proper dams, and lay up a sufficiency of provisions for the winter. They are obliged to cut holes through the ice and snow three-fourths feet thick to cut wood to feed on in the winter. Some of those taken had the skin nearly worn off their feet, and the fur partly worn off their backs, and were so lean from the want and misery they had undergone, that there was scarcely a particle of flesh on their bones. Probably, in severe seasons the most of them die from want, hence beaver never have been numerous here nor are they likely to increase.

THURSDAY [May] 24. Fine weather.

Did not raise camp. Four men, A. Finlay, G. Paris, C. Plante, and F. Champagne, started in the morning to seek a defile to cross the mountains by, and ascertain what sort of a country is ahead them. They are to re-

[300] Sawtooth Mountains.—J. E. R.

[301] At Ross Fork.—J. E. R.

turn tomorrow. Sent after the Indians today again in order to bring one of them to the camp to point out the road, let him be willing or not, but they had fled from where they were yesterday, and it could not be ascertained where they had gone.

FRIDAY [May] 25. Showery after part of the day, and heavy thunder in the evening.

The men who went off yesterday returned, and report that they found a passable road across the mountains but there is still a good deal of snow. On the opposite side there is a pretty extensive valley with a number of small rivers issuing from the mountains, which reunite and form a pretty large stream in the plain below.[302] They set their traps last night, and caught each two beaver.

SATURDAY [May] 26. Cloudy, cold weather.

Proceeded up the river two and one-half hours, seven miles N. N. W.[303] to the entrance of the defile, the road rugged and hilly and mostly through thickets of woods, the river is too high to cross or we would find a good road on the opposite bank.

SUNDAY [May] 27. Heavy rain in the after part of the day.

Started a little after daylight in the morning, and crossed the mountain five and one-half hours, sixteen miles N. N. E. In ascending the road part of the way very stony and nearly covered up with fallen wood. The snow on the height of land and both sides of it compose about the two-thirds of the days journey, on descending we found part of the way very woody and miry.[304] From the badness of the road and the slipper-

302 Salmon River. – P. C. P.

303 South fork Boise River. – J. E. R.

304 Up Vienna and down Smiley Creeks. – J. E. R.

iness of the snow, and horses sinking in it frequently, this was a fatiguing day both on horses and men. The valley appears of considerable extent, the hills on both sides of it partially clothed with pine, the plain below is clear of wood, along the banks of the river small stunted willows which are of too small a size to promise many beaver. All hands were out setting their traps. From traces observed it appears the Americans with some F[lat]head Indians passed this way last summer. A Nez Percés woman who is now with us was along with them. They did not find many beaver. Thus we find the country which we expected to find new and rich is neither, and does not answer the account given of it by the Indians.

MONDAY [May] 28. Heavy rain in the night, showery cold weather during the day. Did not raise camp. All hands visited their traps, and some more were set. Thirty-three beaver taken.

TUESDAY [May] 29. Near a foot deep of snow fell during the night, but the most of it disappeared during the day.

Did not raise camp. The people visited their traps. Sixteen beaver and one otter taken.

WEDNESDAY [May] 30. Fine weather.

Did not raise camp. The people out at their traps. Seventeen beaver taken.

THURSDAY [May] 31. Raw cold weather.

Raised camp, and proceeded four hours, fifteen miles N. N. W. down the river.[305] Four beaver and one otter taken. The road good, a fine plain along the river, hills partially wooded on both sides.

FRIDAY [June] 1. Fine weather.

[305] Down Salmon River.—P. C. P.

Continued our route down the river two hours, seven miles W. We now know where we are. It is on the head of the Salmon River. Mr. Ross returned from here nine years ago, and descended the river.[306] Some of the hunters went a day or two journey farther on.

SATURDAY [June] 2. Fine weather.

Raised camp and proceeded two and three-fourths hours, ten miles W. up another fork.[307] The valley swampy. The river apparently well adapted for beaver yet there is no appearance of any ever having been in it. The hills on both sides wooded with fir. The principal river runs to the north. Twelve men went ahead to a fork which had some beaver in it when Mr. Ross passed here, they are to return tomorrow.

SUNDAY [June] 3. Fine weather forenoon, a violent thunder storm, with a squall of wind and heavy rain afternoon.

Did not raise camp, waiting for the men who went ahead yesterday. They returned. The Americans hunted the fork they went to visit last year. A party of Snakes consisting of three men and three women came to our camp, and traded some leather with the people. These are not so frightened as the last ones we saw, they have encamped along side of us, but we are able to obtain no satisfactory information from them either as to whether any beaver are to be found, or the passes where the mountains can be crossed.

MONDAY [June] 4. Cloudy, fine weather.

Raise camp and proceeded two hours, seven miles

306 Alexander Ross's party, in 1824, came into the Salmon River valley here from the Big Wood River, passing near Galena and descended the Salmon River on return home. – J. E. R.

307 Up Meadow Creek. – J. E. R.

W.N.W. to along a swamp defile across a little height of land to a small creek which runs to the northward.[308] The country has an excellent appearance for beaver but there are none, the little willows are too small. The people out hunting killed some cariboo. Bear tracks are numerous, some which have been killed, as well as cariboo are very lean. A chance track of elk is to be seen. The snow has but recently gone off the ground, it is boggy, and the grass is just beginning to spring up.

TUESDAY [June] 5. Fine weather.

Continued our route four and one-half hours, fifteen miles W.N.W. along a narrow defile and over a mountain not very high, to Charles Fork.[309] The road through thick woods, some banks of snow to pass and in places the ground swampy and boggy. The snow has but very recently gone off the ground, the ground is not yet dry. The grass very short.

WEDNESDAY [June] 6. Fine weather.

Continued our journey three and one-half hours, ten miles W.N.W. Crossed two forks of the river which is very high[310]–lost some of our things. The road very bad the most of the way through thick woods and very boggy. Where we are camped on a little plain the grass is barely beginning to spring up. Two beaver taken. The Indians who promised to accompany us remained behind. Some of the men, ahead on discovery, fell on a river on the opposite side of the mountain which runs to the southward.

THURSDAY [June] 7. Fine weather.

308 Down Trail Creek to south fork of Payette River.–J. E. R.

309 Down south fork of Payette River; thence across hills to Warm Springs Creek.–J. E. R.

310 Fivemile and Clear Creeks.–J. E. R.

Continued our journey three hours, nine miles W. along a swamp[311] and down a steep hill to a river which runs to the southward, it is a fork of Payette's River.[312] The road through thick woods, and very bad. Very little grass for the horses. There have been beaver here some years ago but there are now few or none. Went to the mountains on discovery, great deal of snow. Four beaver taken.

FRIDAY [June] 8. Fine weather.

Continued our journey down the river three hours, eight miles S. Road swampy, through thick woods, fallen timber. Eleven beaver taken. Found a little plain pretty good feeding for the horses.

SATURDAY [June] 9. Cloudy, very heavy rain towards evening.

Proceeded down the river one and one-half hours, four miles, and encamped on a little fork with swampy banks[313] pretty clear of wood in order to find better feeding for the horses. Four men, A. Finlay, Bt. Gadipre, C. Plante, and F. Champagne, crossed the mountain to the westward to another fork[314] to discover a road. They found one which will be passable. Two beaver taken. The people out with their traps. Beaver formerly have been numerous, but at present there are very few. This is a fork of Read's River.[315] Some of our people ascended this fork a few years ago, one of the men, L. Riendeau, knows the place.

SUNDAY [June] 10. Very heavy rain in the night, foggy showery weather during the day.

[311] Deadwood Swamp. – J. E. R.

[312] Deadwood River. – J. E. R.

[313] Ninemile Creek. – J. E. R.

[314] Lightning Creek. – J. E. R.

[315] Middle fork Payette River. – J. E. R.

The unfavorable weather deterred us from raising camp, the trees and bushes were so charged with wet that our baggage would have been completely drenched passing through them.

MONDAY [June] 11. Very heavy rain in the night and forepart of the day.

As yesterday the bad weather deterred us from raising camp. Several of the people out hunting but without success except Kanota who killed an elk. Animals are very scarce here at present, probably owing to the snow having so lately gone off the ground. From the appearance of the old tracks, elk and deer were very numerous here in the fall.

TUESDAY [June] 12. Very heavy rain and in the mountain snow and sleet all day.

The weather faired a little in the morning and we raised camp, and marched four and one-half hours, twelve miles W. across the mountain to another small fork.[316] The road very bad on a succession of steep hills thickly wooded which with the bad weather rendered this a most harassing and fatiguing day both on people and horses. Vegetation is much farther advanced here than on the other side of the mountain. The men who came here three days ago set their traps. Soteau took four large beaver.

WEDNESDAY [June] 13. A perfect pour of rain in the night and forepart of the day.

The bad weather deterred us from raising camp, being delayed this way is much against us as provisions are getting scarce with the people and no beaver.

THURSDAY [June] 14. A pour of rain and sleet in the night and all day.

---

[316] Fork of Ninemile Creek. – J. E. R.

The bad weather again deterred us from raising camp, fortunately our horses have pretty good feeding. Some of the people out hunting but with little success. Animals are very scarce.

FRIDAY [June] 15. Showery during the day.

Raised camp and proceeded down the river and on a range of hills to below where it falls into another large fork, seven hours, twenty-one miles south.[317] The road very bad, through thick woods and over a number of steep hills and deep gullies–where we encamped the woods are becoming clear and the country much better in appearance. Fine feeding for our horses. The river here is pretty large.

SATURDAY [June] 16. A violent storm of thunder and very heavy rain in the night. Showery during the day, heavy rain afterwards.

Proceeded down the river two hours, eight miles S. S.W. to the fork.[318] Here a large river falls in from the eastward. Some of the men who are ahead represent the road along the river as very bad, and a large fork which falls in from the S.W. rolling down between steep banks so rapidly and deep that our camp would not be able to pass it. We have therefore determined to return on our road, and cross the mountains to the westward near our last camp. Several of the people out hunting, but only a cheveau killed, the country has a fine appearance for animals but they are very scarce. Some of the people set a few traps for beaver.

SUNDAY [June] 17. Fair weather.

Crossed the mountains ten hours, twenty-eight miles W.N.W. to a plain.[319] We missed the road, and had a

317 To middle fork Payette.

318 Mouth of middle fork Payette.

319 Big flat at head of Willow Creek.

most harassing days journey on a succession of steep rugged hills and thick woods, and fallen timber. Some of the horses much jaded. Some of the people out hunting, but with little success. Two beaver taken.

MONDAY [June] 18. Fair weather.

Continued our route two and one-half hours, eight miles S. across a plain and a wooded hill, to a large river,[320] which we had to cross on rafts which employed us the remainder of the day. Some of the people are not yet across. This river here runs from W. to E. Some traps were set.

TUESDAY [June] 19. A great deal of thunder and excessive heavy rain in the night. Showery during the day.

The remainder of the people crossed early in the morning, when we proceeded on our journey three and one-half hours, twelve miles S. S. W. on a pretty high mountain but with a good road, and along a narrow, swampy plain. Here we found the Snake Indians[321] with their wives they tell us we are now near the plain. One of the men, Toupe, was obliged to kill a horse to eat, and several others will soon be obliged to do the same, being so long in the mountains and finding no beaver, the people have eaten up all their provisions. Three beaver taken.

WEDNESDAY [June] 20. A pour of rain in the night and all day.

The bad weather deterred us from raising camp.

THURSDAY [June] 21. Excessive heavy rain in the night and rain and snow all day.

We could not stir today either. M. Lefort killed a

320 Big Willow Creek below forks.

321 Wihinast Indians. – J. E. R.

horse to eat. Provisions are becoming very scarce. The Snake chief paid us a visit.

FRIDAY [June] 22. Showery weather.

Raised camp and proceeded across a part of mountain woody, and down several hills to a fork of Payette's River[322] two and one-half hours, eight miles S. S. W. The Snakes are encamped some distance below us, they came to the camp and traded a few roots, and exchanged several horses with the people.

SATURDAY [June] 23. Fine weather.

Continued our journey four and one-half hours, fifteen miles W. N. W. up the river and across a mountain clear of woods to a fork of the Waser River.[323] The mountain steep, the road in places stony, and from the late rain the horses in many places sink very much.

SUNDAY [June] 24. Fine weather.

Continued our route down the fork two and one-half hours, eight miles. We were induced to camp early at the request of a Snake chief who met us, to wait for his people to trade, they encamped on Waser River at some distance.

MONDAY [June] 25. Fine weather.

Did not raise camp. A number of Snake Indians arrived accompanied by three of the chiefs, and passed the most of the day with us, and traded some forty

322 Little Willow Creek. Payette's River named after Francis Payette. Called by Alexander Ross, Payette or Middle River. *Fur Hunters*, ii, 98.–W. S. L.

323 Cave Creek, a fork of the Weiser of today. Variously spelled in early days:–The Wuser River of Alexander Ross, *Fur Hunters*, ii, 98-9, and of Arrowsmeth's maps, and of Charles Wilkes' map of 1841. Wager, Wayers, and Wager's River of Ogden's *Journal* of 1827, Oregon Historical Society *Quarterly*, xi, 362, *ibid.*, xiii, 366. The Wage River in Colonel Albert's map of 1835, also spelled Wagner's River. Presumed to have been named for a Jacob Wayer or Wager, a Northwestern trapper with McKenzie, who first trapped there in 1818.–W. S. L.

beaver, some dry salmon, and changed several horses.

TUESDAY [June] 26. Warm weather.

Raised camp and proceeded six hours, twenty miles S. S. E.[324] The road very stony, and hilly. We are induced to take this road as being the shortest to the big river.

WEDNESDAY [June] 27. Fine weather.

Continued our journey five and one-half hours, eighteen miles S. S. W. to the Snake River about midway between Payette's and Waser Rivers. The road hilly but not so stony as yesterday. The people were set to work immediately and made a skin canoe, to cross the river, but it is not yet dry. The river is very high, and from the steepness of the banks it is difficult to find a good landing place to cross the horses. Some of the people went to a barrier of Waser River, and traded a few salmon. They are very acceptable in our present scarcity of food.

THURSDAY [June] 28. Stormy part of the day.

It was some time in the morning before the canoe was dry and fit for service, it was kept busily employed all day afterwards, yet not more than half the people are across. At the same time the horses were crossed, and much difficulty we had getting them into the water at different times, about twenty are still to cross, all the efforts of the people could not get them driven into the water though assisted by Snake Indians. Some of the people went to the Snake camp in the morning, and traded some and a few dried salmon. Several of the Indians came to the camp, and traded a few beaver and some other articles.

FRIDAY [June] 29. Weather as yesterday.

[324] Should be S. S. W. down Weiser River.

All this day was occupied crossing the baggage. Some of the people are yet to cross. The remainder of the horses were got across except one of the company's mules which was drowned in the traverse.

SATURDAY [June] 30. Fine weather.

The rest of the people got across in the morning, the Budard's [Burdolis] family were crossing the last voyage when the canoe swamped, six people who were in it with difficulty gained the shore, not withstanding the assistance of some of our people, some of the property was recovered but a good deal lost. Sent off eight men, C. Plante as head of the party, F. Champagne, J. Dubruill, L. Quintall, C. Riendeau, A. Masson, P. Grell, and J. Reyhn, to hunt up the river Mathon.[325] The head of the river Sylvank,[326] and six forks of the river chutes.[327] They have twenty-four days to reach the fort. Raised camp and proceeded down the river, two and one-half hours march, eight miles.

SUNDAY [July] 1. Excessive heavy rain in the night and forepart of the day.

It was midday before we could raise camp, when we continued our route down the river and across a point

325 The Malheur River in Oregon. "The Unfortunate River" of Ogden's *Journal*, 1826, Oregon Historical Society *Quarterly*, x, 354. Mr. George H. Himes, secretary of the Oregon Historical Society, who camped at what is now Vale, Oregon, in August, 1853, recalls an old French trapper stating that the river was named "Malheur" on account of some early "misfortune," "loss of goods cached away," or "bad water" encountered by the first trappers along the stream. – W. S. L.

326 Sylvie flows into the Deschutes. The intention was to have Plante's party trap up the Malheur River and cross over to the waters of Crooked River (which flows into the Deschutes) for further trapping and then proceed directly to Fort Nez Percé in the Columbia. – T. C. E.

327 That is, the party proceeded down Snake River along the west bank to the well known place named Olds Ferry and then crossed over the hills to Burnt River at Huntington, Oregon. This was the regular route of the Oregon Trail in later years. – T. C. E.

to Burnt River[328] three and three-fourths hours, fourteen miles.

MONDAY [July] 2. Showery weather in the night and morning.

Proceeded up the river three and one-half hours, twelve miles. Some Indians were encamped at our last station from whom we traded a few beaver.

TUESDAY [July] 3. Stormy, cold, showery weather.

Continued our route up the river to the forks.[329]

WEDNESDAY [July] 4. Raw, cold weather.

Raised camp and proceeded W. S. W. five hours, sixteen miles over a range of rugged hills, and again fell upon the river.[330] Eight men, A. Finlay, L. Kanota, P. Birnie, C. Grosbin, A. Langtin, T. [. . .], J. Toupe, the cook, and some of the families proceeded to hunt on the way to the fort.

THURSDAY [July] 5. Fine weather.

Continued our route up the river three and one-half hours, ten miles W. S. W. Several traps were set yes-

328 Burnt River of Oregon. So called on account of the burnt appearance of the lava formation along the stream. George H. Himes, who walked through the river bottom in August, 1853, with bleeding feet caused by stubbing his toes against the sharp lava rock, is authority for the statement that the stream took its name from the burnt appearance of the lava formations along the water course. Powder River:–This stream derived its name from the powdery, sandy soil along its course, often alluded to by persons–Indians and others–as "polally il lihee"–literally, powdered soil, powdered ground. Our authority is Mr. George H. Himes.–W. S. L.

Polally = gunpowder = black sand. Illihee = soil, ground or country. Chinook.–T. C. E.

329 Followed up Burnt River directly along the Oregon Trail to where Durkee, Oregon, now stands. Here the immigrant road later turned up a creek and ridge to the north but the Indian trail kept westward across the hills to fall upon Burnt River again.–T. C. E.

330 Here the regular Indian trail turned north to the Powder River valley and Grande Ronde and Walla Walla. Mr. Work's party continued up Burnt River, intending to trap the various forks of John Day's River on their way to Fort Nez Percé.–T. C. E.

terday. Eight beaver taken today, and several more traps set. The river has been not long since hunted by the Indians, beaver are scarce, and what few are very lean.

FRIDAY [July] 6. Fine weather.

Raised camp and proceeded up the river W. S. W. eleven miles, three and three-fourths hours. The people out with their traps. One beaver taken.

SATURDAY [July] 7. Fine weather.

Did not raise camp on account of Payette having to examine the road across the mountain to Day's River.[331] One beaver and one otter taken, the hunters out and killed three blacktail deer, there are a few animals along the mountain. Gilbert's horse missing, not known whether stolen or strayed.

SUNDAY [July] 8. Fine weather.

Raised camp and proceeded five hours, fifteen miles W. S. W.[332] across the mountain to a small plain on a small stream which we suppose falls into the southern fork of Day's River. We kept farther to the north than the usual road in order to avoid a steep mountain which is difficult to pass. The road through thick woods and in places hilly and through woods but not very thick. One of the men, Soteaux, went to take up his traps in the morning, and has not yet arrived at the camp. It is conjectured he has gone ahead, and fallen upon the river which is supposed to be close too and set his traps, or perhaps has killed some elk or deer, and

[331] John Day's River of Oregon. Day was robbed here by the Indians in 1811. – W. S. L.

[332] It is impossible to follow closely the road traveled among the streams and mountains of the three forks of John Day's River July 7-17. Their guide had evidently been with Peter Skene Ogden's party in the winter of 1825-6; see Oregon Historical Society *Quarterly*, vol. 10. – T. C. E.

was too late to come to the camp. J. Desland, and L. Riendeau each killed a horse to eat.

MONDAY [July] 9. Showery, very heavy rain in the afternoon.

Raised camp and proceeded down the little fork which is now become pretty large three and three-fourths hours, eleven miles W.S.W. The road through woods and occcasional little plains, in places stony and bad upon the horses' feet. Payette, who is our guide suspects we have fallen upon the head of the north branch of the river. It was winter and eight years ago when he passed, and cannot remember clearly the road. We found a family of mountain Snakes, three men and their wives and six children, and had a few fresh salmon from them and two beaver. They spear the salmon along the river. Some of the men out with the traps. There has been a chance of beaver but the Indians have traps and have been taking them. The people can give us no information, we cannot understand them. No news of Soteaux yet, he probably has fallen on the south fork, and may perhaps be waiting for us.

TUESDAY [July] 10. Showery weather, very heavy rain in the morning.

Owing to the bad weather it was near noon when we raised camp and proceeded down the river three and one-half hours, ten miles W. The river becoming larger as we advanced, but no beaver, tho' in some places it appears well adapted for them. The road through woods and small plains and pretty good though hilly and stony in places. Passed three more families of Indians, only the women and children were in the huts, the men were off hunting. The people traded a few roots from them. Soteaux has not yet come up.

WEDNESDAY [July] 11. Showery weather.

Did not raise camp. We are becoming alarmed for the safety of Soteaux. He has time if he remained to hunt or missed the road to have found it, and come up with us now. Sent four men, J. Faul, Gilbert Ross, W. Gadipre, and Pinet, to seek him. They returned late in the evening, without having seen anything of him. They went to our camp of the evening of the 8. One of them struck across to within sight of another fork which we suppose to be the south branch.

THURSDAY [July] 12. Showery weather.

Did not raise camp. Sent off the men, Faul, Pearce, and Smith, to seek after Soteaux. They are ordered to go on to where he was first missing, to search diligently, and see if they can find any mark of him. They are furnished with good horses, and will have plenty of time to come up with us.

FRIDAY [July] 13. Showery, very heavy rain with thunder in the afternoon.

Raised camp and proceeded down the river one and one-half hours, five miles W. S. W., and then struck across the foot of the mountains two and one-half hours, S. W., eight miles. The road along the river stony and hilly. Along the mountain the road hilly but not many stones.

SATURDAY [July] 14. Showery during the day, very heavy rain in the morning.

The bad weather deterred from raising camp till near noon, proceeded and marched four hours W., five miles to a smaller river, here we found the river so stony and hilly that we had again to ascend the hill, the road the most of the way very stony. The men who started on the twelfth came up with the camp, their horses completely knocked up. They had no intelligence of Soteaux nor could they even follow his tracks. Owing to the recent heavy rain they could with difficulty follow the track of the camp over stony ground.

SUNDAY [July] 15. Heavy rain in the night and morning.

Raised camp and struck out from the river, and marched two and one-half hours, eight miles S. W. and again fell upon the river which we descended two hours, seven miles S. to our road of last year which strikes across the mountains where we encamped, some of the men set a few traps. Several of our horses became lame by the stoniness of the road.

MONDAY [July] 16. Fine warm weather, rain in the night.

Did not raise camp, in order to send five men to the southern fork, where the Snakes have a Wear, to see if they could get any information of Soteaux. They returned in the afternoon; they found the Wear a day's journey nearer than it was last year. No intelligence whatever of Soteaux. Two of the Indians came to the camp in the evening. They are taking no salmon now. Pichette caught two beaver.

TUESDAY [July] 17. Very heavy rain, with thunder in the afternoon.

Raised camp and proceeded six and one-half hours, twenty miles across the mountains. The road in places very stony and bad on the horses' feet.

WEDNESDAY [July] 18. Fine weather.

Continued our route out of the woods and down a little river[333] in the plain four and one-half hours, fifteen miles, the road part of the way stony.

THURSDAY [July] 19. Fine weather.

Came ahead of the camp with a few men and after twelve hours hard riding reached the fort. Where we found Mr. Parker [Pambrum].[334] The men who left me on the 1 inst. Butte River have arrived. They got no beaver. Plante has also arrived, but his party are yet behind. They also got no beaver worth while, they turned back from the head of river Malheur, and did not pass the distance they even decided. They were afraid of not having time, and became discouraged not finding beaver. The report we have among the Snakes regarding our men who descended Salmon River being drowned, unfortunately turns out to be too true, M. Plante and A. Dumois were drowned. L. Biassonette and I. J. B[apis]+[e] were walking ashore their turn, and escaped and reached the fort quite naked.

333 Via Pilot Rock, Oregon, and to the Umatilla River below Pendleton, and from there to Fort Nez Percé by way of Helix and Vansycle. – T. C. E.

334 Bancroft MS. reads Pambrin [Pambrum] who is evidently the person meant, as Mr. Parker did not start on his trip until 1835. Mr. Pierre Crysologue Pambrum, a clerk and chief trader whose name appears as numbers 1178, 977, and 193 on the lists for the years 1821-4. He was a French-Canadian and held a commission in the Canadian forces during the War of 1812 and afterwards joined the Northwest Company. After the coalition with the Hudson's Bay Company he came west of the mountains. He was stationed at Stuart's Lake in 1825; at the Babines in 1830; and came to the Columbia River district in 1831, in which year he was re-engaged as a clerk at £100 a year. He was stationed at Fort Nez Percé, or Walla Walla in 1831, succeeding Archibald McKinley, and continued there until his death. He became a chief trader in 1840 and is frequently mentioned by the members of the Whitman Mission, established in his neighborhood. He was fatally injured, May 11, 1841, by being thrown from a horse which he was riding with a cord, Indian fashion. The cord came out of the horse's mouth, and caused the accident. He was attended by Dr. Marcus Whitman at his death bed. He was buried at Fort Vancouver. – W. S. L.

Everything they had being in the canoe was lost. The unfortunate accident happened when they were just getting out of the bad road. How it happened the survivors could not tell as they did not see it, but found the paddles. The canoe it seems was too small to carry all their baggage and themselves, and they walked along their turn about. They had been descending the river more than thirty days and notwithstanding the account we had heard of beaver they found none. Some Nez Percés Indians whom they fell in with after the misfortune, treated the survivors with the utmost kindness.

FRIDAY [July] 20. Fine weather.

Some more of Plante's party arrived.

SATURDAY [July] 21. Fine weather.

F. Payette and the people whom I left behind two days ago arrived.

SUNDAY [July] 22. Fine weather.

Employed, settling accounts of the people's horses, traps, etc., storing bye their baggage.

MONDAY [July] 23. Fine weather.

Employed as yesterday and had the boats cleaned out ready for gumming.

TUESDAY [July] 24. Fine weather.

Finished gumming the boats, and prepared everything to start for Vancouver tomorrow.

WEDNESDAY [July] 25. Embarked early in the morning thirty men and their boats for Vancouver, and encamped in the evening near Day's River.

THURSDAY [July] 26. Fine weather.

Continued our course early in the morning passed the Chutes and the Dalles portage, and proceeded a few miles down the river and put ashore for supper and men to drive all night.

FRIDAY [July] 27. Drove all night and reached the cascades early in the morning, and arrived at Vancouver in the afternoon.

HORSES 1832

Started from W. W. with	289			
Traded during the voyage	40			329
Lost in the Nez Percés Mountains		23		
Gave up or died on the way in do.		18	41	
Stolen by Blackfeet during the voyage			16	
Killed do. during the voyage			7	
Died during the winter			18	
Gave up or lost etc.			9	
Exchanged two for one			3	
Sold			5	
Killed to eat			8	107
Returned with				215
				322
Not account[ed] for				7
				329

Killed during the voyage three hundred and nine buffalo.

Appendix

Letter from John Work to John McLeod

[KOOTENAY FORT NEZ PERCÉ–COLUMBIA RIV. DIST.[335] COUNTRY] FORT NEZ PERCES
September 6, 1831.

DEAR SIR: It is with much pleasure I have to acknowledge the receipt of your kind favor of 30 July 1830, which was handed me on my arrival from Snake country about a month and a half ago. I was sorry to hear of your ill health, but hope that ere now your visit to the civilised world has completely recovered you. Indeed we had the pleasure to hear from Captain Kipling that you were well before the Ganymede sailed from London. I envy you the pleasures you have enjoyed of civilised life, which I have so long deprived myself of. I fear the seclusion of our Indian life with its want of comfort or anything like enjoyment will be very irksome to you.

My last campaign in the Snake country was not so successful as I had anticipated, the returns and profits were nevertheless pretty fair considering the exhausted state of the country and the great severity and unusual length of the winter, which was greatly against our trapping operations. Moreover we met some parties of Americans who had hunted over portions of the country through which we meant to pass. I escaped with my scalp last year. I much doubt whether I

335 Not in Work's handwriting.

shall be so fortunate this trip, I am now just starting for the borders of the Blackfoot and F[lat]head lands, a much more dangerous part of the country than wh[ich] we passed last year, my party is too weak for the undertaking, but from the sickness prevailing at Vancouver no more men could be spared but as this is the only quarter now where there is a likelihood of making anything we must try. The country to the southward is ruined so much that little or nothing is to be done in it–an intermittent fever was raging at Vancouver wh[en] I left. This scourge was carrying off the few wretched natives who had escaped it last year, it had also attacked several of the people about the establishment. My people did not escape it. Several of them were taken ill, and some of them remain so badly that I am obliged to leave them here, as they are not able to proceed, this I much regret as my numbers at first were too weak.

Before this reaches you, you will have had all the Columbia news, I need therefore not trouble you on this subject.

Wishing you my every manner of happiness, I remain my dear sir, Yours sincerely and truly,

JOHN WORK[336]

JOHN MCLEOD ESQR.

[336] Original in Canadian Archives.

Letter from John Work to Edward Ermatinger

FORT VANCOUVER, 5 August 1832

MY DEAR EDWD. On arrival from the Snake country a few days ago I was much gratified by the receipt of your two most welcome, highly esteemed, and interesting letters dated 4 August and 8 December 1830. It gives me particular pleasure to hear that you were hearty and well and had at last fairly got under way in business with good reason to entertain hopes of succeeding well. You will no doubt my friend meet with some difficulties, and experiences, some vexing and untoward occurrences at the commencement, let me entreat you not to allow these to discourage you, persevere and there is no doubt prudence and assiduity will eventually command success. Heaven's grant that the time may soon come that your success may equal your most sanguine expectations. I am happy in being able to inform you that I enjoy good health, and am yet blessed with the possession of my scalp which is rather more than I had reason to expect. This last my friend has been a severe years duty on me, all my perseverence and fortitude were scarcely sufficient to bear up against the danger, misery, and consequent anxiety to which I was exposed. My difficulties commenced at the very offset, on leaving this place the fever attacked the people and they fell off so fast that every boat was like an hospital, and I really thought at one time that I would not be able to reach N[ez] Percés however at last I got that length, where I left a few of the sickest of the men and proceeded on my route, and after unusual difficulties in crossing the mountains by a new road we arrived on the borders of the Blackfoot country, these barbarians immediately fell upon us and allowed us no respite but kept continually hanging round us. We had different battles with them which I regret were attended with bloodshed on sundry occasions but six men and an Indian killed, and some more wounded. On the thirtieth January we had a hard battle with a powerful party of them, on this occasion I received a slight wound in the arm. Several of the scoundrels fell also. They were so numerous I was able to make no hunt. I have not had the pleasure of seeing Frank [Ermatinger], but had a letter from him, he had left N[ez] Percés a few days before I arrived, he tells me he did not agree well with Mr. Hern [Francis Herron, chief trader] at Colville last winter, and he had a serious dispute with Mr. Black during the summer. He has given me very little news from my old quarters Colville. There is a great change here since you left. You would be astonished to see the quantity of ground under cultivation and the immense crops which they have, the season has been favourable. The vessels are employed to the northward under Mr. Ogden [Peter Skene Ogden, Chief Factor] who is procuring a few beaver skins at most exorbitant price, there is a very strong opposition. Mr. [Duncan] Finlayson, now a C. F. came in here last fall, he is now off on a voyage to the islands so I have not had the pleasure of seeing him. It appears our worthy chief the Dr. [John McLoughlin] leaves us in the spring, which I much regret. He continues as assiduous as ever to every branch of the business. There is an increased bustle about the place. I am going to start with my ragmuffin freeman to the southward towards the Spanish settlements with what success I cannot say. I am tired of the cursed country, Ned, and becoming more dissatisfied every day with the measures in it; things don't go fair, I don't think I shall remain long, my plan is to hide myself in some out of the way corner, and drag out the remainder of my days as quietly as possible. Susette is well, we have now got three little girls, they accompanied me these last two years, but I leave them behind this one, the misery is too great. I shall be very lonely without them, but the cursed trip exposes them to too much hardship. I, last year, wrote to a brother that I have at a place called Monkton in New Brunswick, directing him to look out and perhaps enter into business at the same time offering him what I could spare of the needful, and if prospects are fair I would go and join him. What think you of the plan? You will most likely see our friend [John] Todd, he has gone out last spring to visit the civilised world. Persevere, my friend and may God prosper you, Adieu: Your ever affectionate friend

JOHN WORK

MR. EDWD. ERMATINGER.

P.S. Inform me how you are getting on, what prospects a person like me would have, in different branches, particularly farming, and what capital would suffice in a middling and high scale, and the society, manner of living, and other particulars, in your quarter.

J.W.[337]

337 Original in Provincial Library, Victoria, B. C., Canada.

Original Letters of John Work to Edward Ermatinger

(1) Colville, January 2, 1828.
(2) Colville, March 28, 1829.
(3) Flat Heads, March 19, 1830.
(4) Fort Vancouver, August 5, 1832.
(5) Fort Vancouver, February 24, 1834.
(6) Columbia River, December 13, 1834.
(7) Columbia River, January 1, 1836.
(8) Fort Simpson, N.W. Coast, February 15, 1837.
(9) N. West Coast, America, February 10, 1838.
(10) Fort Simpson, September 10, 1838.
(11) Steamer Beunee, October 24, 1839.
(12) Fort Colville, March 5, 1841.
(13) Fort Simpson, October 11, 1841.
(14) Fort Simpson, February 15, 1841.
(15) Fort Colville, March 30, 1842.
(16) Fort Simpson, February 6, 1844.
(17) Vancouver, November 14, 1846.
(18) Nisqualley, January 10, 1846.
(19) Fort Vancouver, November 23, 1847.
(20) Fort Victoria, November 9, 1848.
(21) Fort Victoria, December 10, 1849.
(22) Fort Victoria, March 14, 1853.
(23) Victoria, Vancouver Island, August 8, 1856.

A Bibliography of the Fur Trade in the Northwest

AMERICAN FUR COMPANY.

1. Blotter, April 1, 1817, to May 13, Montreal: June 15 to October 6, 1819, Michilimackinac.
2. Journal, April 1, 1817, to September 20, 1834.
3. Journal, Northern Michilimackinac April 19, 1827, September 15, 1832.
4. Invoices Outward, C, Northern, 1830-1834.
5. Ledger, April 1, 1817-September 20, 1834.
6. Ledger, Northern, 1827-1834.

These six volumes are now in the Canadian Archives, Ottawa, Ontario, and are apparently all that remain of the papers of the American Fur Company under the administration of John Jacob Astor.

AMERICAN FUR COMPANY, Papers from 1834-1848.

This is practically a complete collection of the papers of the American Fur Company under the administration of Ramsey Crooks. They are now in boxes in the New York Historical Library.

BANCROFT, HUBERT HOWE. History of the Northwest Coast. (San Francisco, 1886). 2 volumes in *Works*, volumes xxvii and xxviii.

BANCROFT, HUBERT HOWE. History of Washington, Idaho, and Montana (San Francisco, 1890). In *Works*, volume xxxi.

BIGGAR, H. P. Early Fur Trading Companies of New France. In University of Toronto, *Studies in History*, 1901.

CHITTENDEN, HIRAM MARTIN. American Fur Trade of Far West (New York, 1902). 3 volumes.

The standard history of the American fur trading companies operating east of the Rocky Mountains. It contains a vast amount of detail and is almost documentary in character.

CHOUTEAU, AUGUSTE. Collections, in Missouri Historical Society, St. Louis.

CHOUTEAU, PIERRE. Collections, in Missouri Historical Society, St. Louis.

The Chouteau papers contain a vast quantity of material concerning the fur trade.

COMAN, KATHARINE. Economic Beginnings of the Far West (New York, 1912). 2 volumes.

COUES, ELLIOTT. (Editor). Manuscript Journals of Alexander Henry, Fur Trader of the Northwest Company and of David Thompson, Official Geographer and Explorer of the same company, 1799-1814. (New Light on the Early History of the Northwest, New York, 1897). 3 volumes.

COX, ROSS. Adventures on Columbia River, including narrative of residence of six years on eastern side of Rocky Mountains (New York, 1832).

DALE, HARRISON CLIFFORD. Ashley-Smith Explorations and the Discovery of a Central Route to the Pacific (Cleveland, 1918).

Particularly valuable for the operations of the Rocky Mountain Fur Company.

DAVIDSON, GORDON CHARLES. Northwest Company (Berkeley, 1918). In University of California *Publications in History*, volume vii.

The standard account of the Northwest Fur Company.

DELAND, CHARLES E. The Verendrye Explorations and Discoveries. In South Dakota *Historical Collections*, volume vii.

DODDS, JAMES. The Hudson Bay Company, Its position and prospects, Substance of address delivered to shareholders, 1866 (London, 1866).

DOUGLAS, DAVID. Journal kept by David Douglas during his travels in North America, 1823-1827 (London, 1914). Published under the directions of the Royal Horticultural Society.

DRIPS, ANDREW. Papers. In Missouri Historical Society.

DUGAS, GEORGE. The Canadian West: Its discovery by the Sieur de La Vérendrye, its development by the fur trading companies down to the year 1822 (Montreal, 1905). Translated from the French.

DUNN, JOHN. The Oregon Territory and British North American Fur Trade (Philadelphia, 1845).

ELLIOTT, T. C. David Thompson, Pathfinder, and the Columbia River, (Kettle Falls, Washington, 1911).

ELLIOTT, T. C. The Fur Trade in the Columbia River Basin prior to 1811. In Washington Historical Society *Quarterly*, 1915.

ELLIOTT, T. C. Peter Skene Ogden, Fur Trader. In Oregon Historical Society *Quarterly*, volume xi.

FITZGERALD, JAMES EDWARD. Examination of Charter and Proceedings of Hudson's Bay Company with reference to grant of Vancouver's Island (London, 1849).

Contains many interesting letters and statistics otherwise unavailable. Hostile to the Hudson's Bay Company.

FRANCHERE, GABRIEL. Narrative of Voyage to Northwest Coast of America, 1811-12-13-14, or the first American settlement on the Pacific (New York, 1854).

Reprinted in Thwaites, *Early Western Travels* (Cleveland, 1904), volume vi.

GEBHARD, ELIZABETH L. Life and Adventures of John Jacob Astor (Hudson, N. Y., 1915).

GOLDER, F. Russian Expansion on the Pacific, 1641-1850. Account of the earliest and later expeditions made by Russians along the Pacific coast of Asia and North America (Cleveland, 1914).

GREAT BRITAIN: COLONIAL OFFICE I: volume i, no. 2. Reports of Ye Contrie Sr. Humfrey Gilbert goes to discou. Copy in Canadian Archives, Ottawa, Ontario.

GREAT BRITAIN: HOUSE OF COMMONS. Report from the Select Committee on Aborigines (British Settlements) with the minutes of evidence. Ordered by the House of Commons to be printed 26 June, 1837.

GREAT BRITAIN: HOUSE OF COMMONS. Report from the Select Committee on the Hudson's Bay Company, together with the proceedings of the Committee, Ordered Printed by the House of Commons 31 July, and August, 1857.

GREAT BRITAIN: COLONIAL OFFICE. Return to an Address of the Honourable The House of Commons dated 26 May, 1842: for copy of the Existing Charter or Grant by the Crown to the Hudson's Bay Company: together with Copies or Extracts of the Correspondence which took place at the last Renewal of the Charter between the Government and the Company, or of individuals on behalf of the Company: also the Dates of all former Charters or Grants to that Company. London, Ordered by House of Commons to be printed, 8 August, 1842.

HALL, JAMES. Statistics of the West at close of year 1836 (Cincinnati, 1836).

HARMON, DANIEL WILLIAMS. Voyages of a Partner in the Northwest Company, 1800-05 (Andover, 1820).

HENRY, ALEXANDER. Travels and Adventures in Canada and the Indian Territories, 1760 and 1776 (New York, 1809).

HOLMAN, FREDERICK V. Dr. John McLoughlin, the Father of Oregon (Cleveland, 1907).

HUDSON'S BAY COMPANY. Statement of Commissioned Officers. In Canadian Archives, Ottawa, Ontario, M 865.

JAMES, THOMAS. Three years among Indians and Mexicans, by General Thomas James of Monroe County, Illinois: edited by Walter B. Douglas (St. Louis, Missouri Historical Society, 1916).

LAROCQUE, J. P. Journal of Larocque from the Assiniboine to the Yellowstone, 1805 (Ottawa, 1910). Edited by L. J. Burpee in Report of the Canadian Archives Commission.

LAUT, AGNES CHRISTINA. Conquest of the Great Northwest (New York, 1918).

LISA, MANUEL, Letter Book, in Missouri Historical Society.

MACKENZIE, ALEXANDER. Voyages from Montreal through the continent of North America to Frozen and Pacific Oceans, 1789-93. With account of rise, progress, and present state of fur trade of that country (London, 1801). Reprint 2 volumes (New York, 1912).

McKENZIE, CHARLES. Journal of a Second Expedition to the Mississouri [sic] 1805 in *Masson Collection.*

McLEAN, JOHN. Notes of a Twenty-five Years' Service in the Hudson's Bay Territory (London, 1849).

McLEOD, JOHN. Journals. In Canadian Archives, Ottawa, Ontario.

MASSON, LOUIS, F. R. Les Bourgeois de la Compagnie du Nord-Ouest (Quebec, 1889-1890). 2 volumes.

MORICE, ADRIEN GABRIEL. History of Northern Interior of British Columbia (Toronto, 1904).

ORIGIN AND PROGRESS of the Northwest Company, London, 1811. *Masson Collection* V.
Pamphlet.

OGDEN, PETER SKENE. Traits of American Indian Life and Character. By a Fur Trader (London, 1853).

PAPERS RE BRITISH COLUMBIA. Copies in Canadian Archives, Ottawa, Canada.

ROSS, ALEXANDER. Adventures of First Settlers in Oregon or Columbia River (London, 1849). Reprint in Thwaites, *Early Western Travels* (Cleveland, 1904). Volume vii.

ROSS, ALEXANDER. The Fur Hunters of the Far West (London, 1855). 2 volumes.

SCHAFER, JOSEPH. History of the Pacific Northwest (New York, 1918).

SELKIRK, EARL OF. Sketch of British Fur Trade in North America with observations relative to Northwest Company of Montreal (London, 1816).

SIMPSON, SIR GEORGE. Letters, 1841-1843. In *American Historical Review* (New York, 1908). Volume xiv.

SIMPSON, SIR GEORGE. Overland Journey Round the World, during years 1841 and 1842 (Philadelphia, 1847). 2 volumes.

SKINNER, CONSTANCE LINDSAY. Adventures of Oregon. In *Yale Chronicles of America* (New Haven, 1920). xxii.

A well written but superficial narrative.

SUBLETTE, WILLIAM L. Papers in Missouri Historical Society.

Four envelopes containing the papers between 1830-1850.

THOMPSON, DAVID. Narratives of his explorations in Western America, 1784-1812. Edited by J. B. Tyrell (Toronto, 1916). *Publications of Champlain Society*, volume xii.

THWAITES, REUBEN GOLD. Early Rocky Mountain Explorations (New York, 1904).

TREXLER, HARRISON A. Buffalo Range of the Northwest. In *Mississippi Valley Historical Review*. Volume vii, no. 4.

UMFREVILLE, EDWARD. The Present State of Hudson's Bay containing a full description of that settlement . . . and likewise of the fur trade, with hints for its improvement . . . (London, 1790).

WILLSON, BECKLES. The Great Company: being a history of the honourable company of merchants – adventurers trading into Hudson's Bay (Toronto, 1899).

WORK, JOHN. Journals. Originals in Provincial Library, Victoria, British Columbia. Copies contained in thirteen folios in Cartons labeled H. B. C. British Columbia and Vancouver, 1823-1839, in Canadian Archives, Ottawa, Ontario. Cartons labeled

"Received from Mr. Gosnell, Archivist. Victoria, B. C., November 20, 1908.

There are also some copies in Bancroft Collections. These are not so accurate as Mr. Gosnell's copies.

WYETH, JOHN B. Oregon or a Short History of a long journey from the Atlantic to regions of the Pacific by land in Thwaites *Early Western Travels* (Cleveland, 1905). Volume xxi.

WYETH, NATHANIEL. The Correspondence and Journals of, 1831-6. A record of two expeditions for the occupation of the Oregon country (ed. T. G. Young). In *Sources of the History of Oregon* (Eugene, Oregon, 1899). Volume i, parts 3-6.

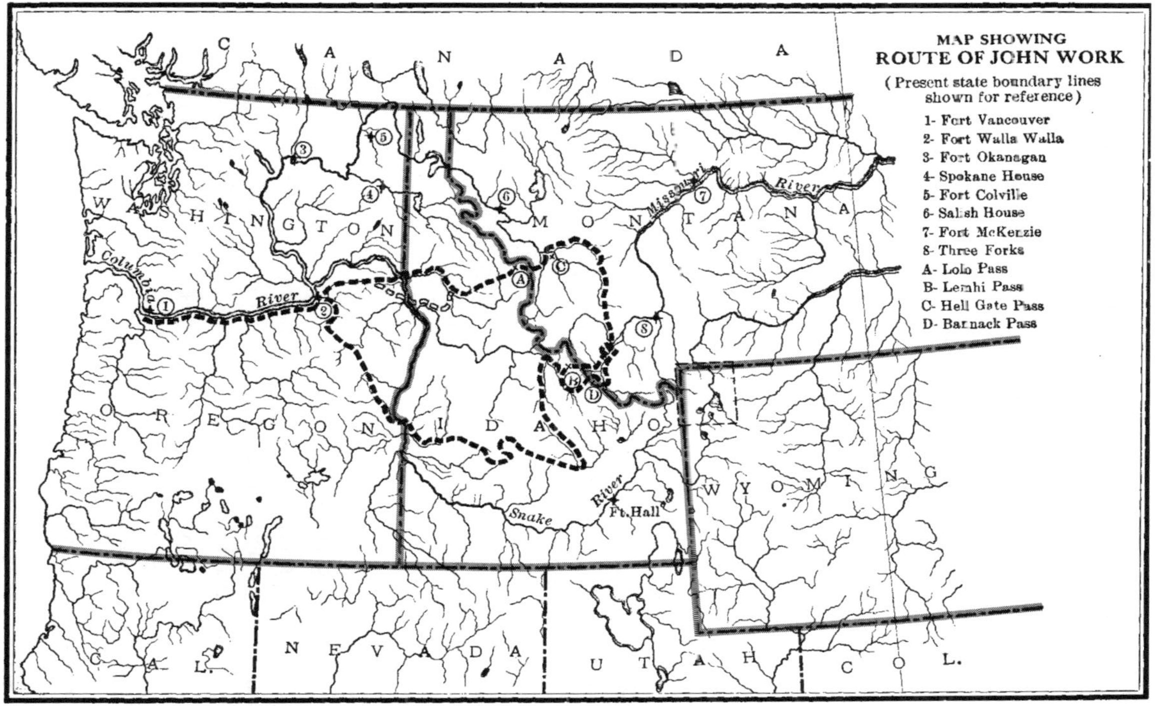
MAP SHOWING
ROUTE OF JOHN WORK
(Present state boundary lines shown for reference)
1- Fort Vancouver
2- Fort Walla Walla
3- Fort Okanagan
4- Spokane House
5- Fort Colville
6- Salish House
7- Fort McKenzie
8- Three Forks
A- Lolo Pass
B- Lemhi Pass
C- Hell Gate Pass
D- Bannack Pass
CANADA
WASHINGTON
OREGON
IDAHO
MONTANA
WYOMING
NEVADA
UTAH
CAL.
COL.
Columbia
River
Missouri
River
Snake
River
Ft. Hall

Index

Index

This book is a
complete reproduction
of *The Journal of John Work*.
No text has been omitted.